ON THE MARGINS OF THE WORLD

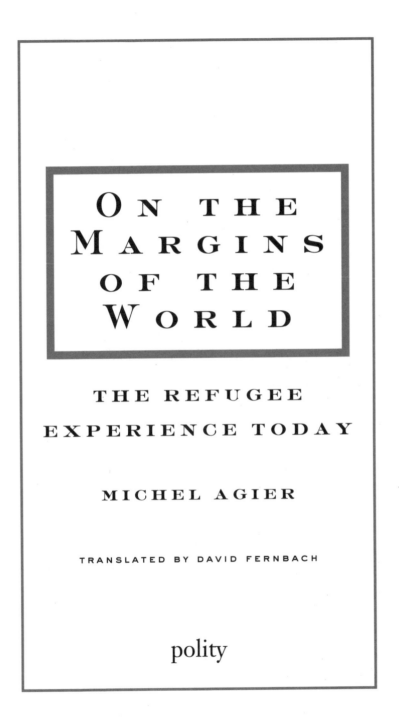

ON THE MARGINS OF THE WORLD

THE REFUGEE EXPERIENCE TODAY

MICHEL AGIER

TRANSLATED BY DAVID FERNBACH

polity

First published in French as *Aux Bords Du Monde, Les Réfugiés*
© Editions Flammarion, 2005

This English edition © Polity Press, 2008

Polity Press
65 Bridge Street
Cambridge CB2 1UR, UK.

Polity Press
350 Main Street
Malden, MA 02148, USA

ISBN-13: 978-07456-4051-8
ISBN-13: 978-07456-4052-5 (pb)

A catalogue record for this book is available from the British Library.

Typeset in 10.75 on 14 pt in Adobe Janson
by Servis Filmsetting Ltd, Manchester
Printed and bound in India by Replika Press PVT Ltd, Kundli

For further information on Polity, visit our website: www.polity.co.uk

Ouvrage publié avec le concours du Ministère français chargé de la culture
– Centre National du Livre

Published with the assistance of the French Ministry of Culture
– National Centre for the Book

CONTENTS

PREFACE TO THE ENGLISH EDITION

I planned this book as a set of reflections designed to establish some preliminary markers for an anthropology of the social worlds of war, exile and humanitarian aid. But it also developed into an alarm call, directed at a larger audience than just the academic milieu.

To alert public opinion, in this case, does not mean making supposed 'revelations', still less denouncing 'scandals'. This kind of thing tends rather to provoke a paralysis that only confirms our preconception of this other world, its character suddenly revealed as 'unacceptable' and 'intolerable'. The task here is to make it understandable. We need to think through this unconsidered aspect of the state of the world, if we are to imagine and assist the transformation of these placeless spaces, these social worlds created by violent conflict, these chaotic socio-political states and forced displacements, and the way that so many of the world's population are left waiting on the margins of the world. The 'part of those with no part', as Jacques Rancière put it, in other words those left behind and excluded from the distribution of goods, spaces and powers. A residual space of wasted lives, the production of which is marked by what Zygmunt Bauman has described as a culture of rejection that is inevitably bound up with any modernizing obsession: a wholesale banishment of undesirables that accompanies economic, political or territorial re-ordering. The question that I raise on this basis is whether these people will remain without a voice, or whether their space of an outcast life, however strange it might be, could be transformed into a site of social life and political expression, thus also transforming its victims, whom we still perceive as more or less guilty or undesirable, into recognized subjects with a kind of citizenship in practice.

The work therefore aims to alert, inform and raise some signposts for understanding, rather than scandal, denunciation or rejection. For one factor in what Michel Foucault called 'outdoor imprisonment', the banishment of refugees and other of the world's economic, political or social outcasts, is precisely maintaining those who do not share this fate (i.e. 'we', writers and readers, decision-makers and donors) in our condition of spectators, with only a passing experience of unusual paralysis. This kind of paralysis is disconcerting, and provokes reactions guided by emotion: compassion, fear, moral accusation, racist rejection. In all cases, banishment (displayed very clearly by present European and North American politics towards foreigners from Africa, Asia and Latin America) is shored up by an intellectual distancing, a misrepresentation in which these worlds are maintained as, or transformed into, realities that are irreducibly 'other'. This frozen otherness is established today in the thinking and practice of the countries of exile, and is the basis of all rejection – racial, cultural and xenophobic. As opposed to this, the deeper work of scholarship, the slow discovery of the complexity of different lives, finds here its most political meaning: it denotes an experience of anthropology that consists not in exhibiting irreducible differences, but rather in reducing their alterity.

This *slow discovery* is what matters, the present work being only a milestone towards it. In fact, faced with emergency demands that authoritatively rule out any time for reflection, it is both possible and necessary to base a divergent and critical discourse on examples drawn from investigation and reflection, a discourse rarely heard in the public sphere. This displays the various logics, both global and local, that give rise to and reproduce these margins of the world, as well as the challenges and transformations that intersect them in the very sites of confinement.

Michel Agier
October 2006

INTRODUCTION

We notice them sometimes on the outskirts of our cities, sometimes at the gap in their fabric: in sheds, on parking lots, at roundabouts and beneath bridges – the last extensions of a country outside our vision, the scattered representatives of an extreme world. These women with their children who look so out of place in the urban context, and whom we seek uneasily to avoid: Turkish survivors of a shipwreck arrested in a Mediterranean port, or arrivals from Afghanistan or Iraq who have spent weeks at sea, between two ports and two countries on a ship on the Indian Ocean; recent wanderers, true or false refugees, illegal immigrants, all waiting for the strangers who don't understand them to decide one day on their status.

As soon as this bruised population makes its appearance, fear, compassion and blame jostle together with their cargo of blinding stereotypes: a world of victims, dirty like the wars that have produced it, a violent and unjust world in which people kill each other for no reason in some far-off place.

But who are they all, surviving and squatting at the edge of our lives and our gaze? How did they get here? Have they forfeited all humanity, if we feel so little touched by them?

Across differences of continent and nationality, religion and language, fifty million people today have fled war and violence. They find themselves placed, for long periods or forever, at the outer limits of life – physical, social, political and economic – almost dropping out of the common space that should naturally connect all human beings.

International news offers us fresh examples every day, even if the events of 2001 thrust to the centre of contemporary history many of the phenomena described in the present book. The attacks of 11 September and the American response in Afghanistan that followed before the year end multiplied the scale and destitution of this 'country' of refugees. An immense flow of exiles abroad and displaced people internally was expected: more than three million according to the forecasts of UN agencies. These forecasts proved excessive, but they were readily understandable in the light of an established fact rarely cited in the media, which was bound now to be aggravated to an unforeseeable degree: as a result of the twenty years of conflict that their country had already experienced, three and a half million Afghans had fled their country as refugees (mainly to Pakistan and Iran), and at least a further million were displaced internally. On top of these we must add the countless 'invisible' refugees, not officially declared as such, who have sometimes been able to return or reach relative safety,[1] but are often pursued as illegal immigrants on the seas of the Far East or attempting to cross the borders of Europe, somewhere between Turkey, Sangatte and Dover.

The world of the displaced and refugees has been created before our eyes, or at least in our own time: the result of dirty wars, terror, the brutal stripping bare of individual life,

flight and the formation of new refugee camps, illegality and
the spectacle of nameless victims. All these things have long
affected the Afghan people, most often outside our field
of vision, as well as the peoples of Somalia, southern Sudan,
Chechnya and Colombia, not to mention those 'historic'
refugees, the Palestinians, who have spent years in their
camps to the ups and down of an interminable war. They are
all emblematic of a human condition that is shaped and fixed
on the margins of the world, one of its most tenacious foundations being our own ignorance of it.

This book grew out of a study I began in 1999 on peoples in
exodus in the wars of sub-Saharan Africa and Colombia, and
aims to give a view and understanding of the process by which
a section of our common planet is today being put in quarantine.[2] It mingles observations that intersect and respond to
one another, personal stories, viewpoints, on-site descriptions
and portraits. Psychologists and psychiatrists emphasize the
traumas of war, flight and exile, and the care that each individual victim would need to restore them fully to life. Political
and geopolitical studies, for their part, reveal the games of
power and especially territory that fuel so many wars, of varying intensity but all outside any rules, and often deliberately
provoking massive transfers of population. These approaches
are indispensable and indeed find their way into the present
book, but there is also another dimension revealed more
directly by the anthropologist's insight and reflection: the existential context that all inhabitants of this strange 'country'
share. Afghan refugees, displaced people in Colombia, victims
of repression in the Congo, Rwandan deportees – all have
experienced exodus, an experience whose meaning appears
more clearly if we approach it in its three stages – the found-
ing moments of a new kind of wandering life.

First of all, the stage of destruction – land, houses and
towns ravaged by war, as well as the broken trajectories of

lives and the irreducible mark of physical and moral wounds. Then that of confinement – months of waiting, years or whole life-cycles spent in transit on the fringes of cities or in camps that seem trying to become towns without ever managing to do so. Finally, the moment of action, still uncertain and hesitant: the search for a right to life and speech which, in the disturbed contexts of war and exodus, often emerges in a context of illegality, but may eventually give birth to new forms of political commitment. These are three sequences of the same existential context, so interwoven that to ignore one of them means losing the sense of the whole and making way for the resurgence of fear, suspicion, and finally violence towards the illegal and disturbed exile, arrested and sent back 'home' when this home disappeared long ago.

In describing these three stages of refugee identity, the present book seeks to reveal the universal dimension of this phenomenon, which is in no way ethnic or particularist. It is a literally *anthropological* aim, in the sense that it questions our understanding of what it means today to be human.

No difference in language, religion or skin colour is responsible for the arbitrariness and violence of the crimes, exclusions and de-humanizations that mark the wars and exoduses of today, horrifying and scandalizing us. As against the ready-made 'truths' we are given to think, it is necessary rather to start from the social situations and experiences that are lived and shared, to trace the chain of lost causes buried in complex political histories. Often, the strangeness of a situation is due to the fact that recent layers of unresolved conflict have superimposed themselves on others that are older and less visible, without suppressing these. Accumulated in this way, they have combined to steadily worsen social life, and obscured or killed off political processes. The result is a simultaneity and multiplicity of causes, of a violence that some end up deeming 'without cause'. While this may be wrong, many examples attest to an extreme logic with no longer any apparent solution, its components being the absence of a negotiated solution along with the impunity of political criminality, the spread of weapons and the many-sided activity of illegal networks.

Threatened by war and the social degradation this provokes, the identity of civilian populations becomes a vital problem. If they escape a death with no apparent reason, if they manage to flee the theatre of a conflict that has become senseless for them, these human beings on reprieve and merely surviving make perfect victims. Strange as it may seem to me, their life then reveals a part of myself, of my own humanity: every human being, placed in this situation of exodus, waiting and non-definition must recompose themselves from a basis of destitution. By grasping human identity at the sites of its denial, we inquire more directly into its foundations: this is the revolt of life in contact with death; it is what they call in Colombia a peace built in the midst of war, a home that is imagined throughout the exodus.

To recognize the specific experience of this many-coloured and multi-ethnic population in its most universal feature in no way means separating it off under the pretext of some new difference. It means on the contrary making possible and urgent its reinsertion into the human world, despite and against all the 'specific' wars that produced it. Such a project may be universalist and ambitious, but its realization demands nothing more than providing the simplest and most modest means of socialization: health care, work, shelter, and access to education, something far less costly than the resources deployed to manufacture the instruments of warfare and imprisonment.

What do we need to do, if we want to direct our gaze, our concern, our commitment towards the actual situations in which the world of refugees is created? The spectacle of human drama played out on the television screen makes this less authentic, by having to compete with other images that confuse us by their semblance of reality: family sitcoms, sporting contests, or false 'survivor' stories. The European hostages on the island of Jolo, for example, filmed daily throughout their captivity in summer 2000, were forced to protest several times against the media amalgamation that transformed them despite themselves into heroes of a TV soap.

Words can help us understand, by reintroducing nuances that the images lose, as long as they are precise enough to describe from within what actually happens, what is actually lived. To speak of sufferings while criticizing the victimization of which refugees are the object. To understand the ambiguity and defilement of identities formed in and through violence, without falling into discourses of accusation and suspicion. And in this way also to understand how refugees and displaced people can find a new social place, a *humanity*, in collective action, the only condition by which they can shed their identity as victims.

2

BRUISED POPULATIONS

A WHOLE COUNTRY OF VICTIMS

In the early 1950s, when the United Nations had recently assumed responsibility for refugees on a global scale, their number was assessed at something over one and a half million. These were the result of the Second World War, the flight from Eastern to Western Europe, and the birth of the state of Israel, and they were concentrated in Europe and the Middle East.

Half a century later, the United Nations High Commission for Refugees, established in 1951, qualifies some fifty million people as 'victims of forced displacement'. Between twelve and eighteen million of these are refugees in the strict sense, i.e. now living outside their country of origin, and massively concentrated in Africa (seven to eight million) and Asia (over six million), along with the three million Palestinians who have been refugees in various Middle Eastern countries since the 1940s or 1960s. Slightly over three million of these refugees are in the process of a repatriation organized by the UNHCR. Finally, twenty-five to thirty million more people, in its estimation, have experienced forced displacement within their own country, in the wake of internal violence and warfare; these include 800,000 in Burundi, a million each in Sri Lanka, Angola and Afghanistan, two million in Colombia, over three million in the Sudan, and large numbers in many other countries.[1]

Fifty million 'victims of forced displacement' add up to a whole country defined by one common feature, the humanitarian description of 'victim', a population reduced to the sole imperative of keeping alive far from home, in places of waiting. Nothing more. An unknown people that no one knows what to do with, human beings who have become both victims and undesirables. To patch up the social fissures that perpetuate, renew and expand this phenomenon is increasingly difficult.

These fissures are first of all the exoduses triggered by looting, sacking and destruction of every kind – human, material and environmental. Flight becomes the only chance of survival: the hasty departure of townspeople who have survived the 'cleansing' of their quarter, suddenly isolated or orphaned; the collective march of peasant families gathering together as they flee war, each feeling a certain protection from the presence of others.

These millions of forced displacements, these quests for refuge in another country, are provoked by the generalization and spread of local wars that have gradually taken the place of the wars between the great powers. The Cold War concealed local conflicts for a long while, offering them an ideological cover in lieu of a deeper sense, and above all it dominated the political and military systems of the regions in conflict.

Once freed from this political and ideological vice, wars became more unpredictable than ever, as well as more disparate and numerous: the dawn of the twenty-first century saw about thirty raging simultaneously. They added to causes of forced displacement that were already at work and often just as violent: the devastation of land, famine, illegal prospecting for gold and precious metals, or the building of dams on the land of indigenous peoples. It is frequently the case, as in Ethiopia in 1984 and Somalia in 1991, that natural catastrophes and murderous conflicts combine to multiply famine and displacement.

Each war waged across the world today is thus the result of multiple causes: social wars and urban revolts of wretched people left behind by development, ethnic wars that conceal the interests of diamond mining or petrol companies, revolutionary guerrilla wars that have long since lost contact with any social movement, Islamist rebellions that combine the grievances of a region abandoned by a too distant state. Any of these causes may have been good in its time, before being petrified and perverted into a bad cause for want of dialogue; in some cases, where the conflict has not brought results and for lack of any other solution, combatants from each side have become professionals of permanent warfare.

Then there are those wars termed 'dirty' because instead of regular armies fighting one another, a legal army fights an illegal one, or armed groups oppose civilian populations – between 70 and 90 per cent of the victims of internal conflicts are civilians. They are also known as 'low intensity' wars, as the scale of military operations fluctuates. Other forms of warfare have also developed: kidnapping of civilians, the murder of popular leaders or elected representatives viewed as 'military targets', attacks on the heart of cities, collective massacres of villagers, expulsions *manu militari* of the inhabitants of coveted regions, etc. These generally find little resonance in the media, and except when European tourists or journalists are kidnapped, the killings, atrocities and expulsions are generally conducted away from the global gaze, with no impact on international life. They make every kind of pillage possible: looting of shops and houses by attackers who are hungry themselves, or economic looting on a larger scale, of natural resources such as diamonds for example, by foreign companies that are more or less legal, some of them also controlling arms sales to regions in conflict. Others find it that much easier to grab land in a situation where terror reigns and despoliation passes unnoticed.

The professionalizing of militias and the generalization of violence have transformed the conditions of war and exodus: the same private armed groups act sometimes in the name of the state, sometimes against it, sometimes in the context of war and sometimes in that of common criminality, without it being possible any longer to distinguish a priori what kind of actor or motivation one is dealing with. In such different situations as Ireland, Colombia and Indonesia, for example, the ideological leaders of guerrilla wars have become increasingly isolated within their own political movements. Either impotent or complicit, they observe the strength of the ties that their 'armed branches' make with criminal gangs, going on themselves to take the initiative in kidnapping or looting that is now dressed up in political or religious discourse. Sometimes, as in Cali in Colombia, criminal gangs undertake kidnappings that they then sell on to armed groups which claim them as hostage taking.

It is only possible to account for the existence of a margin of the world common to all survivors if we discount – at least provisionally, in the first instance – the rhetoric of good and bad causes. At the end of the day, a new population is being formed out of this confusion, this mixture of impasse and rejection, these wars that never come to an end. A single population but not a homogeneous one, made up of individual trajectories of wandering and humiliation, long stays in marginal zones and transit camps, experience of a fragile and uncertain relationship to the law and to states – those that have expelled them and those that have accepted them. It is an inexpressible world because it has no definable borders – although largely produced in the political sphere when this fails in governing society. A shameful residue of unsuccessful conflicts, it is thus a *post-political* world in its origins. Lacking the homogeneity of ethnicity or party, the world of refugees is a political encumbrance in each country where it arrives. Just to speak of it is disturbing for the listener and uncomfortable for the speaker. The words needed lack a proper place.

THE FATE OF LEÓN MONTAÑO

One terrible day in 1997, León Montaño left his house and land on the Pacific coast of Colombia, together with his wife, their children and grandchildren. The war had reached them. 'It's impossible to work if you're afraid', he said, then fell silent. His wife, for her part, obsessionally repeated her own fears. The *guerrilleros* had taken over the village opposite their farm, on the other bank of the river. They had never met them. Like many farmers displaced by internal warfare in their country, they confused soldiers and paramilitaries, the 'self-defence' groups of the far right and the guerrillas of the left. They also spoke of the soldiers who had burned coca fields a little upstream from them – not their land, they insisted, as they didn't grow coca. For many years León Montaño had cut and sold wood: later the family had lived from selling charcoal, fishing, and the plantains that they grew.

When the war caught up with them, they 'decided' to leave. Two of their children had already settled in the suburbs of Cali, the third city in Colombia with a population of two million. Their eldest daughter lived in an '*invasión*', an illegally occupied urban site settled by migrants who were overwhelmingly poor, many of them black, and had arrived from the Pacific coast since the mid 1970s. León hastily sold the land and small house that the family possessed for 200,000 pesos (around 100 euros / $135), after living there for thirty years; another plot he simply abandoned. The journey to Cali cost a quarter of their savings, and the rest was gone after a few weeks. A poor peasant in his sixties, León rented one room for his entire family, close to the eldest daughter. Three months later he found himself with neither work nor money. One day he noticed a 'free place' at the end of a dirty alley: 'I put a plastic sheet up and we slept there', he said. That is where they have been ever since. The spot has become their hut, their *rancho*, made of black plastic, boards and hurdles. That is where I first met them in 1999.

The hut shelters fifteen persons, including their two adolescent daughters and their baby. They have a reputation among the young people of the quarter as being very 'rural', a bit simple. For food they all go out looking for remains at the market, and beg. They voice no demands, and have no plans. That is the biggest difference between them and the other poor people in the quarter. The important thing for León Montaño is to be accepted by their neighbours in the alley, and at the nearest medical station; to be recognized as victims. They are led to break the law in order to survive. Their life is accordingly marked by fear of the police and the armed gangs who carry out 'social cleansing'. Their destitution seems total: social, psychological, economic – a total absence of social activity, almost permanent isolation in their hut, with begging their only recourse. They are at once *victims*, *illegal*, and *defenceless*. If they differ at all from any of the others who make up the world of refugees today, it is that these three characteristics, instead of being distinct and successive, affect them at one and the same time and place.

The following year I saw them again, in the same hut made of branches and black plastic where the parental couple had gone to ground. They seem on the point of abandoning our common reality. León, his head bent down, has a distant air and was constantly mumbling. His wife, fixed on a folding chair at the dark entrance to their shelter, begs with gestures and cries, and has given up any concern for her appearance. The people of the quarter show them neither hatred nor respect.

Their expression is engraved in my memory and still intrigues me today: had they already quite abandoned our world and passed into another, their own, engendered by distress, incomprehension, a permanent feeling of persecution – a world in which sudden gestures and cries replace the faculty of speech? I have kept the conviction, ever since, that it is possible to demonstrate point by point, step by step, that their 'madness', a loss of social existence, was avoidable. We can show this by focusing on something whose vague existence we are all aware of without daring to approach it, either from fear or hypocrisy, scrutinizing the forms of decomposition and recomposition of the simplest and most elementary human identity, that needed by anyone, anywhere, to keep alive: a place, social ties, the right to speak.

This encounter was like a call to know more, to let the first emotions slowly give way to questions, doubt, an entire process of reflection. Why had these people succumbed when others managed to 'remake' themselves? We would have to mention the death of their daughter (the one whom they came to Cali to stay with) when her house was set on fire by criminals in revenge for local people – including herself – fending off a militia attack. Another factor would be the brutal suddenness of this unwanted migration with its train of children and grandchildren, lacking home, work, even documents to prove their status as displaced persons. Again, the absence of any emergency facilities, even though they did receive a minimal aid of 10,000 pesos a fortnight, about 5 euros ($7), from their eldest son, who lived in another outlying quarter and worked in construction. And I should also say that Fernando Murillo, a social worker for the district committee who accompanied me, was shocked by their condition even though he was very familiar with this particular '*invasión*' in the poorest zone of the quarter.

We then set out to find other displaced people. Three years earlier, an inquiry by the Catholic church's 'Truth, Justice and Peace' commission had counted over a hundred in this zone of illegal habitation with its population of some two and a half thousand. The majority of these however had disappeared: whether they had returned to the countryside, melted more securely into the town, were hiding in a shack in a different shanty-town, or had been murdered by the local private militia.

On a world scale, this family is nothing. Just one family among the millions of a strange 'country' made up of escapees and survivors of violence and exodus. Day after day, wars without end have decomposed all social life in the countries they affect. In the Balkans, in Chechnya, Turkey and Colombia, in the Great Lakes region and the Horn of Africa, in Algeria, Tibet and Timor, the absence of a solution to the 'little' wars under way for so many years, sometimes decades, perpetuates precarious situations, and the people displaced become eternal wanderers. Once their houses, districts, villages or towns have been abandoned, their temporary regroupings, whether in camps isolated from everything or on the margins of other cities, become permanent even while still perceived as temporary. As these provisional situations multiply, they end up engendering a new form of being-in-the-world, characterized by wandering and lasting destitution – or rather, a form of *no longer being* in the world, for a certain time or for ever.

LESS ALIVE, LESS HUMAN

Terms such as 'displaced' and 'refugees' say nothing about an essential fact: first of all these people escaped a massacre, fled from direct threats to their lives, surviving by chance the bombardment of their village, the machine-gunning of their building, or the destruction of their town.

Mogadishu, Grozny and Sarajevo were destroyed to wipe out all material traces, all indications of identity, of the population under attack. Collective identities, sites of identity and the bearings of daily life were destroyed or ruined at the same time, leaving no other alternative but flight.

In Sarajevo in 1994, fires and the destruction of monuments expressed 'in the panicked minds of the city's destroyers' a hatred against the city itself, in the sense of the relations of urban life.[2] The war against the town also destroyed the town as space of citizenship, of politics, and thus of resistance to war. Eventually, the destroyers even broke up the minimal symbols of community: material goods, those little emblems of social status; the familiar environments of building, apartment and street, where people spend the day, where they have their familiar routes and meeting-places; monuments as supports of memory and collective identity. These are the destroyed symbols of a commonplace identity that lies at the basis of the everyday humanity of each inhabitant.

In Colombia, to be a *desplazado* or *desplazada* is essentially to have experienced an event placed between the human and the non-human. For many people, it means having suffered or witnessed acts of dehumanization, such as are particularly practised by the paramilitary organizations in their work of 'cleansing' villages and regions by eliminating the guerrillas who control these and their supposed accomplices.

Survivors testify to the meticulous conduct of certain massacres, with their victims being treated by their torturers as animals – 'pigs' or 'chickens'. When they take possession of a village territory, this involves a visual demonstration of the submission of the humiliated inhabitants: the mutilated corpses of relatives, friends and neighbours are hung or lined up on the ground in full view. Their death has reduced them to a non-human state, but the object of this process is to sully the survivors: it forms the shameful identity of those who have witnessed such foul forms of killing but remained alive.

Testimonies related from Chechnya and the Chechen refugee camps in Ingushetia by Anna Politovskaya in 1999 demonstrated a state terrorism perpetrated against the non-combatant civil population.[3] The refugees who arrived in Ingushetia were 'welcomed' and guarded by Russian mercenaries under the control of the Ministry of Justice rather than by the regular army. These are actually groups of ex-prisoners who had regularly been involved in repressing prison riots. Their excesses against Chechen civilians were well known to the administration. These 'legal bandits' as Politovskaya calls them, violent men recruited as soldiers, were the first intermediaries that the refugees had to deal with, placing them from the start in a world of humiliation and lack of rights.

The inhabitants of Grozny, for their part, experienced or narrowly escaped the 'cleansing' of districts and suburbs of the town effected by soldiers; collective massacre or rape followed by murder and very often the decapitation of the victim, sowed terror among the survivors. The soldiers 'did not confine themselves to killing people', the author relates, 'but humiliated and tortured them'. Just as with the Colombian paramilitaries, their 'cleansing' was a meticulous *dehumanization.* This violence, which sought to do more than just kill, affected anyone who was supposed, not even to be in contact with the Chechen fighters, but simply to share with them a certain identity, according to a very summary evaluation of genealogical or territorial proximity.

In the diversity of these distant wars – all local, specific, and apparently resistant to generalization –, there is a common initial act that it is important to grasp and bear in mind: that of sullying the victims, making them not simply less alive (wounded or dead) but also less human.[4] Like the fighters of the 'Revolutionary United Front' in Sierra Leone, who in their last offensive after being evicted from power in 1998, systematically cut off the arms or hands not just of adults, but even of children and babies supposed to belong to the enemy camp. As if this act of irreversible mutilation, beyond the palpable intoxication and craziness of the murderers, was to mark its victims and so naturalize right away their submission, obtained simply by an absurd and precarious superiority of weapons. Another indication is the strange vocabulary that paramilitary commandos and other private bands of ethnic or social 'cleansing' have invented as names for their murderous collectives, a global inventory of which is still awaited: Birds, Horses, Scorpions and Chameleons in Colombia; Cobras, Hawks and Condors in Central Africa; as well as ancient or modern monsters such as Dragons in the Philippines, Ninjas in central Africa, Algeria or Indonesia. Those who carry out this dirty work and keep dirty wars running first of all transform themselves into transmitters of inhumanity. Seduced by a fictional world in which dreams of power and realities of war are confused, and seamlessly passing from the exploits of Rambo and other Exterminators to the orders of their actual warlords, they hurl themselves into their massacres drugged and masked as if in an dream, but a dream which they know very well is a lie, their butcheries being only too real.

In certain countries – Chechnya, Guatemala, the Philippines and Indonesia, among others – those who wield power have had recourse to various kinds of 'death squads', 'popular commandos' or 'self-defence groups'. Whether they directly encourage these or support them, the states in question thus privatize a part of their repressive apparatus, leaving the governing personnel innocent before the law and in the face of international public opinion. But the control of these private armies often escapes them; the commanders themselves can become victims. The state is then privatized by the battling factions, seized, instrumentalized and diluted as simply another stake in the war.

The notion of 'state terrorism' then becomes meaningless. For the very meaning of the state is lost in these successive privatizations of violence and repressive institutions. The horror of the paramilitaries and the dehumanization of their victims are direct effects of this deregulation of war.

NOT KNOWING WHY

Do we know who is who among today's combatants? Do these wars have any meaning for the millions of refugees, and how do they see the different battling factions? Are they innocent victims? Is it possible to be innocent amid these 'dirty wars'? Are there spaces of safety in the generalized violence, oases of peace amidst suspicion and terror? All these questions are faced by the civilian populations of Algeria, Indonesia, Colombia and Sierra Leone, wherever old political conflicts have been fixed and frozen into habits and minds, becoming the *context* in which people are born, marry and work.

In Colombia, a general climate of morbid anticipation is palpable throughout society. Political violence goes back to the division of spaces of power between the two official parties, Liberal and Conservative, in the late nineteenth century. The great *violencia* of the 1948–64 period saw battles between the political militias of these two parties that brought the death of 200,000 people and the forced displacement of many hundreds of thousands more. A far-left guerrilla movement developed in the 1960s, in reaction to the exclusive division of power finally agreed between the two main traditional parties. Twenty years later, having lost a large part of its popular anchorage owing to its exactions, and with the disarmament of certain other groups, this movement had become both isolated within Colombian society and consolidated as a large and powerful warring enterprise. The two leading guerrilla groups – FARC (Revolutionary Armed Forces of Colombia) and ELN (National Liberation Army) – grew in power thanks to their close ties with organizations that produce and distribute drugs ('narco-traffic'), their levies on rural local administrations, large plantations and the national petroleum company, as well as thousands of kidnappings for ransom. They have managed to train substantial armies – with a total of some 20,000 soldiers in 2000, including a large number of unemployed adolescents – and equip themselves with sophisticated weaponry. In parallel, the formation of paramilitary groups has been the result of the development of 'peasant self-defence' against the guerrillas, generally underpinned by the army, as well as underground squads made up in part of regular soldiers, ex-soldiers or policemen that carry out murders of a social or political character (known as *limpieza*, 'cleansing') that the army and police are not able to conduct openly.

In the course of the 1990s, the illegal armed groups (guerrillas and paramilitaries) professionalized themselves both territorially and economically, with a major development of narco-trafficking, whilst the state and the regular army lost a large part of their credibility in maintaining order and territorial control: 822 out of 1,050 local districts in the country, i.e. over 78 per cent, had a greater or lesser guerrilla and/or paramilitary presence in the year 2000, with an estimated 40 per cent of the national territory to be deemed under the control of illegal armed groups.

The complexity and diversification of the conflict today are such that its initial causes are buried under the ashes of hundreds of destroyed villages and tens of thousands of corpses. Omnipresent yet undeclared, the war terrifies all citizens and faces them daily with problems of safety, even if life is not endangered in the same way in towns and in villages, rich and poor quarters, by the guerrillas and by the paramilitaries. The sites and points of entry for violence are multiple, and no one can be sure to escape it. The central place of terror means a narrowing of possible social spaces.[5]

It is in this context of uncertainty and terror that everyday practices and projects, such as 'decisions' to move, are taken. Between 1985 and 2000, two million people in Colombia were displaced by violence, or nearly 5 per cent of the country's total population.[6] The respective share of responsibility for forced displacements of the different groups involved in the armed conflict (paramilitaries, guerrillas and army) varies substantially from one year to the next and from one region to another. Today the war is largely steered by struggles for regional or local control of economic territories and resources – banana fields, palm groves, coca plantations. The farmers and inhabitants of small rural settlements may flee first from the arrival of the guerrillas and then from that of the paramilitaries. The national statistics for forced displacements thus change from year to year, from one department or town to another, without any settled pattern being detectable, and this enables everyone to make their own judgements and forecasts.

In 1996, the paramilitary organizations were held responsible for 33 per cent of forced displacements across the
whole country, but this rate drops to 13 per cent for those
displaced persons who reached Cali. In the same year, the
various guerrilla groups are supposed to have provoked the
flight of 29 per cent of the *desplazados*, but again only 21 per
cent of those reaching Cali. Intervention of the army and
police, finally, led to 16 per cent of *desplazados* on the
national scale, but only to 8 per cent for those registered as
arriving at Cali that year.

A particular feature of Cali is that it is a centre of urban
militias, which are stronger here than in other Colombian
towns. In the course of the same year, 1996, these provoked
the forced displacement – within the city, but to other
quarters – of 23 per cent of the population, whereas urban
militias are 'only' responsible for 6 per cent of forced displacements nationally.[7] At Cali more than elsewhere, the war
has penetrated part of the town: urban sections of national
guerrillas can be found there, as well as several armed criminal gangs (the *pandillas*), and along with this, 'social cleansing' (*limpieza*) gangs, nuclei of self-defence groups that can
run paramilitary 'crusades' or convert themselves into drug
dealers. Violence runs in a network, circulating between politics, society and economics.

A similar confusion is met with in other regions of Colombia. Some organizations manage to pass from one camp to the
other. This was the case with the EPL (Popular Liberation
Army) guerrilla of Maoist inspiration, which after its official
'reintegration' in 1991 became linked to the army and paramilitaries, under the name of Esperanza, Paz y Liberdad.
Individuals frequently change camps: thus, when the paramilitaries move into a zone, they recruit former *guerrilleros* who
use their experience to establish lists of villagers who have col-
laborated with the guerrilla movement. These unfortunates,

with no chance of claiming innocence, are dragged from their homes and immediately killed by the paramilitaries, if they have not managed to take flight in time.

Uncertainty rises, and fear spreads throughout daily life. The groups or 'causes' that immediately triggered displacement are no more than particular signs of the history of violence in the village or quarter in question, or even in a particular family – the fruit of individual perceptions that are often confused, but by which each person in turn tries to make sense of a fate that is now collective and national.

It is in the context of this confusion between armed groups and combatants that social characters of a new type have emerged, like the 'sobel' in Sierra Leone. In 1991, when the RUF (Revolutionary United Front) was created, it mobilized from the start young adolescents recruited from marginalized social milieus, with the object of overthrowing the government of the day. The government followed suit. Thousands of young people were thus socialized by a war that went on for six years. The pay of fighters in the government army was meagre, so they complemented this by pillaging or seizing goods already taken by the rebels. The rebels, for their part, got their arms and uniforms from government soldiers that they killed. The point soon came when the villagers could not tell the difference between all these young soldiers – or even if they did not confuse them physically, they saw little difference between their attitudes. Anyone who wore a uniform and carried a weapon was a 'soldier by day and rebel by night' – hence, 'sobel'. The term entered popular language during the Sierra Leone war.[8]

In the long run, political and social violence end up fuelling one another thanks to the direct or indirect interconnection, immediate or slightly delayed, of several armed networks. According to the country in question, these networks may be organized gangs of thieves, assassins, groups set up to conduct social or ethnic 'cleansing' (protected by the police, if not actually made up of camouflaged policemen), or former prisoners converted into security guards. All of these are trained or reproduced within pro-government armies, paramilitary groups, or political militias. Violence spreads throughout society, and the forced displacement of the civilian population multiplies for reasons that seem to have nothing immediately to do with the war: displaced people expelled from quarters under militia control, or from land invaded by drug traffickers, join with those who have directly fled from guerrillas or paramilitaries, and are confused with them.

The dirty wars have introduced something new into the lives of their victims. For some of them this means not knowing why, for what idea, they are killed or wounded, perhaps not knowing even by whom; for others, it means not knowing why, for what crime, they have to flee their homes so precipitously. If death is thus even more absurd and inconceivable, each person is frightened to perceive that their own survival is uncertain, to see all the possible meanings of the experienced situation disappear. By reducing more each day the spaces of freedom, meeting and dialogue, wars that are not only dirty but also undeclared and increasingly 'senseless' slowly suppress political life, social life, indeed life of any kind.

THE UNNAMEABLE SUFFERING OF EXODUS

Exodus in war is not a simple migration from one place to another. It is best to make clear right away that refugees are not migrants. Not only have they not chosen to be on the move, but their exile actually prolongs the violence, massacre and fear that provoked it in the first place and redefined their most intimate personal identity, which is attacked, injured and bruised. The multiple troubles of unregulated war then continue with their repercussions on the exodus itself, bringing interminable complications in their wake. The original suffering, formed by the emotional personal experience of destruction of places, goods and human beings, is then deepened in the course of a trajectory wandering, a wounding existence.

Each of these itineraries is punctuated by physical and psychological wounds, by interminable days of walking, by hunger, by the death or disappearance of parents, siblings or spouses, by movements of collective fear and panic, by the search for shelter and still more so for a hiding-place. Membership of a large ethnic group can make it easier to extricate oneself from certain legal or economic impasses, help recognize and 'repair' the consequences of exile; but even this resource, though far from negligible, in no way lessens individual suffering. And if this is later expressed by each person in their own particular way, it is because there are a thousand ways to be human, not just one. It is enough that the survivors speak of these moments of violence and exodus for the memory of suffering to resurface, and find new expression in lamentations, *youyous* and other ritual expressions, or in silence, tears or gestures. Even if this suffering is later the object of commentaries and customs, or indeed instrumentalized for political, ethnic or other purposes, it has existed and must be told and described.

The exodus of refugees today is no longer that of the political exiles of the 1930s, 1940s or 1950s, from Spain, Poland or Hungary, who carried with them a powerful ideological message and a sense of personal honour. Far from glory of any kind, it is an accumulation of losses, rejections and flights, of family, administrative or material imbroglios, the only outcome of which, for those who experience it, is to have themselves accepted as victims and receive emergency humanitarian aid, or to live clandestinely. Even so, we only meet the survivors.

We are in one of the three refugee camps at Dadaab, in the dry north-east of Kenya. Opened in 1991–2, these sheltered some 124,000 refugees in June 2000. In his round hut, made like the Soomaali nomadic tents (or *aqallo*) of a scaffolding of bent wooden poles supporting bound branches, but in this case covered by the blue-and-white plastic sheets of the UNHCR, Fartoun tells of her flight from Mogadishu in 1991. She says that they lived well in the Somalian capital, her husband even says that they were rich. He had a small hotel and restaurant, which was destroyed along with half of the city by the bombs of the civil war.

The militias, acting in the names of the Raxanwyen and Hawiye clans against the dictator in power since 1969, General Siyad Barre, hunted down and killed people of different factions of the Darood clan, allied to the regime and held responsible for the social sufferings of everyone else. Then in 1991–2 conflict broke out between sub-clans within the Hawiye faction, after this took control of Mogadishu. Within the overall Soomaali ethnic group, classification in terms of clan membership combines the various levels of personal identification, from the large confederation (*tol*) down to the extended family (*reer*). An identity is achieved between two or more people when they share one of the possible proper names: a family name, a clan name, or that of a confederation. This is an inclusive genealogical mode of recognition, effective in a nomadic milieu: wherever people are, proximity and solidarity can operate. Thus within the Waranle confederation, the Darood and Hawiye clans can intermarry.

But the same clans can also fight one another, as the identification procedure can also be a mode of differentiation and even rejection of the other, from the level of major clans (such as Darood and Hawiye) down to the narrowest level, that of the extended family. The exclusive mode intervenes when the social tensions of a moment, bound up for example with the authoritarian exercise of power, access to land, water and provisions,[9] do not find a solution and are expressed in terms of inherited identities held to be essential or 'natural': genealogical, 'racial', etc. Patrilineal clan identification then becomes an excluding and caricaturing political differentiation: a key to persecution, with frozen and fetishized identities leading to assassination by Kalashnikov and flight.

So Fartoun fled Mogadishu in one direction and her husband in another, along with their baby. Certain escapees claim that, because of the system of patrilineal filiation, women – who do not transmit social kinship – have been less affected than men by persecution and butchery on grounds of identity.

They abandoned everything, got hold of vehicles and left in a hurry. They met up again some thirty kilometres along the way, and continued together to the town of Kismaayo, further south. Their second child was born here. Then the same militia arrived at Kismaayo and chased them away: Fartoun, her husband and two children, as well as the husband's 'brother', also a Darood, who had taken them in. 'There were thousands of people who fled, some left naked', she says.

Another Soomaali refugee, Ali, living today in the same camp and working as a volunteer for a clinic of Médecins Sans Frontières, was about twenty years old when he fled Mogadishu, alone, at the same time as Fartoun and the others. He relates that on the way out of the capital he was caught by the militia. He made a run for it. Without money, with nothing to eat, he did not stop for eighteen days until he reached the Kenyan border. Like him, Fartoun and her family crossed the border and reached the camp at Liboi, just on the other side. There the UNHCR gave them a ration card, a blue-and-white plastic sheet, and cooking utensils. They stayed three years in the same UNHCR tent, three years with nothing to do.

Bandits made incursions, and Somalian militias often crossed the frontier, entered the camps, found out family names and clan membership, killed people and then left. In 1994 the UNHCR closed this camp, as being too close to the border and thus too dangerous.

An identical problem arose at the same time in the Walda camp in northern Kenya, near the Ethiopian frontier. Here it was the army of the new regime in Addis Ababa, established after the civil war of 1990–1, that expelled families of civil servants and soldiers who had worked for the previous government, that of the notoriously cruel and cynical dictator Mengistu. These families were moved in 1993 to the other major Kenyan camp, that of Kekuma in the north of the country, which presently has 50,000 inhabitants. But owing to internal conflicts among the Ethiopians, some of these were transferred a year later to Dadaab. The responsible UN officials admit today that refugee camps have to be established, for security reasons, at least fifty kilometres from a border.

The Somalian refugees at Liboi, like those at Mandera, another Kenyan camp on the border with Somalia, were thus transported by lorry to Dadaab, a hundred kilometres from the frontier. Fartoun and her family now found themselves in the Ifo camp, one of the three UNHCR sites at Dadaab: 'This is your land', they were told, 'you can establish yourselves here.'

This was the itinerary taken by tens of thousands of Somalians at the same time, leading them from the cities of Mogadishu and Kismaayo, and the rural zones in the south of the country, to reach the Dadaab camps at a greater or lesser delay. Some of them arrived as early as 1991; Fartoun reached there in 1994, after transfer from a border camp; others arrived in 1995, coming from camps established four years earlier on the shore of the Indian Ocean near the port of Mombasa; others, finally, came in 1996 from the camp at Tika, fifty kilometres from Nairobi. The risks bound up with proximity to the frontier, the conflicts within the camps and the decision of the Kenyan government to stop establishing camps near large towns, were factors favouring the regroupment of the refugees at Dadaab on the one hand, and Kakuma on the other, both in the north of the country. Ethiopians, Sudanese and Ugandans underwent comparable prolonged trajectories of flight and displacement. On top of these shifts of population were the permanent flows of refugees from cities where they had lived clandestinely: Nairobi, or Garissa, the chief town in the district which included the Dadaab camps.

Each displaced person, each refugee, carries within them the experience of being undesirable and placeless. A lived experience of the original act of violent persecution, then the trials and complications of exodus, resented by governments that refuse to register or assist populations displaced within their own country. Other governments, more or less obliged to let refugees arrive on their soil, refuse to give them a national status as refugees, and try to negotiate their departure with international organizations.

Because their exile has already come up against the resistance of neighbouring countries, the 'internally displaced' form the most numerous category of deportees, the least protected as well as the fastest growing.[10] They are not officially included among the populations assisted by the UNHCR, though this does try to count them, while the countries in which they are found, themselves in internal war, either refuse to protect them or are impotent to do so. A relative stagnation in the number of refugees exiled in another country from one year to the next, or even a decline, is not in itself a sign of any improvement, but rather that of an absence of political and legal response adapted to the destitution of civil populations in the face of internal warfare, hence an aggravation of the overall situation.

MELTING AWAY, HIDING, DISAPPEARING

It is often hard to locate people displaced by force, to meet them and have a dialogue. This is because displaced people seek to melt into the population as discreetly as possible, because they survive in conditions of economic or general illegality that confine them to silence, or because as refugees in camps they are kept at a distance by the security services. This reveals the sole characteristic that unifies this entire population scattered across the planet: displaced people and refugees find themselves for a time placed outside the *nomos*, outside the ordinary human law. Their existence is based on the loss of a geographical place, to which were attached attributes of identity, relationship and memory, and likewise on the absence of any new social place. Let us dwell for a moment on the gap thus created in the life of each refugee – a gap made up of distance and waiting.

In the suddenness and confusion of forced displacement, each of them has experienced an inconceivable moment in their own life. At the same time, they have received without wanting it a collective identity defined as the simple undesirable residue of wars: shameful, clandestine or hunted, this is an identity imposed under constraint and lack of community, in other words without a specific place or culture that give it a foundation. Any community of interest, such as becomes necessary as soon as exile persists and action has to be taken in order to survive, must thus be conceived in conditions that are particularly hostile, marked by ethnic, social or political heterogeneity, and by the devaluing of this new identity in the eyes of others.

For the immense majority, who have to survive in a situation of waiting, displacement represents a brutal entry into a state of liminal floating, without their knowing whether this will turn out to be temporary or lasting. Hence the many terms used today to designate these populations in different countries: 'displaced', 'dispersed', 'deported', 'escapees', 'repressed', 'returned', 'damaged', 'expelled', and so on, suggesting for the most part a movement that is incomplete, in suspense, an instant and a condition that are midway between a point of departure and an inaccessible end point, either of arrival or return. 'Refuge' itself denotes a temporary shelter, while waiting for something better.

The states of apathy and depression, expressions of aggressiveness or intolerance, that are noted by psychologists in displaced persons, come back to this lack of definition, and ultimately to a more or less lasting space-time of anomie: a life without *nomos*, with no stable law to integrate their fate into that of humanity in general. The absence of projects – individual, familial or community – is a further aspect just as typical of this lack of law. The decomposition of families can be observed not only on the occasion of displacement itself – domestic groups often break up, or departure leads to the death of a family member – but also on that of arrival: the fragility and sometimes the insecurity of everyday relations in the new context leads to separations, the dispersion of children, and conflicts. In these extreme contexts, the scope of family solidarity is substantially reduced: thus at Cali, in Colombia, relatives in the poor quarters where the *desplazados* arrive facilitate only an initial contact with the city – little more than do neighbours.

Indeed, those already there are themselves badly housed, scarcely protected in economic terms, and poorly defended against violence.

Not everyone who wants to becomes a town-dweller. A new urban cinema has already explored this depths of this exodus: a cinema of destitution (*The Promise*, *Rosetta*, *La Vendedora de Rosas*),[11] which shows the town in its seamy side, from the perspective of those men and women who have no rights. 'You will not fall into the pit. I will not fall into the pit', the adolescent Rosetta repeats before falling asleep. She lives in an encampment, a 'campsite', in a caravan that does not move.

All energy that is left is focused on a strategy of mere survival, physical and biological, to protect and feed oneself in the absence of any project for life. For how long can this persist?

PHYSICALLY DEFILED, MORALLY SUSPECT

The long and contradictory construction of the world of refugees, in which murderers and victims, 'guilty' and 'innocent', rub shoulders, where suspicion reigns, produces the image of a population with a double blemish: physically defiled and morally suspect.

In Colombia, the heterogeneity of the category of displaced persons reflects the character of the violence itself. Among them can be found ex-*guerrilleros* as well as paramilitaries and their sympathizers, both sides still occasionally active in urban groups; criminals fleeing their former accomplices and 'social cleansing' militias who have been temporarily recruited from criminal elements; peasants terrified by news of the arrival of guerrilla war, who have abandoned house and land, and those who have fled the repression of the army because they gave in to the brutal orders of the drug traffickers to grow coca on their fields. In the media and in popular rumour, compassion yields very soon to suspicion as soon as an attempt is made to say who the displaced are. They come from places defiled by war, places that no one wants to know.

Prejudice assumes the existence of individual or 'categorical' stains on the part of displaced persons contaminated by the massacres, violence, treason and forced complicity that were the causes of their displacement. In the same spirit, the idea develops that an entire geographical region whose population has been the victim of violence has become a 'sick member' of a continent, of the 'body' of Europe, as the writer Ismaïl Kadaré observed in relation to Kosovo.[12] The body of this Europe has to be amputated of the diseased limb.

These contemporary imaginaries of stigmatization and physical alteration reproduce the terms of hygienism, and further back, of racial thinking, typical of the nineteenth century, which is where the idea of segregation springs from. Putting the human body in direct relationship with the politics of space, segregation was attributed from the start a prophylactic function, vis-à-vis the supposed risk of close contact with populations that were biologically or culturally different, terms interchangeable in the mind of that time. With an ambivalence that is found again today in the treatment of refugees, the segregation of diseased or weak populations aimed to protect them from the superiority of the surrounding society as well as to protect the dominant society from possible contamination by different groups, weak or abnormal. This twofold justification had already been put forward in the late sixteenth century, in the context of an alliance between the colonial power and Catholic missions to establish *resguardos*, reserves of indigenous populations in the Spanish and Portuguese colonies of the New World.

In an extreme form of conceiving difference, whether racist or ethnicist, the frontier is the site of a risk of contamination or 'pollution' of identity. Segregation is thus an extreme form of relationship to the other, placed at the ultimate limits of their negation, just before their disappearance. Carmen Bernand[13] has very effectively introduced into reflection on segregation the arguments of Mary Douglas[14] on 'pollution' and the symbolism of the threat of blemish. Modern Western societies still display a continuing belief that associates dirt, and more generally impurity (biological, moral or identitarian) with all kinds of margins: polluted shores are polluting, thus frontiers must remain impermeable, this is what the prophylactic rhetoric of segregation essentially maintains. In this representation, impurity and disorder, non-being and death are placed 'at the confines of society, and opposed to what remains under the society's control; these inarticulated regions are thus margins and confused limits beyond the frontiers'.[15]

The reproduction on a world scale, illustrated time and again in the media, of the categories of order and disorder, the pure and the impure, the clear and the dirty, has succeeded today in building a genuine symbolic wall, no longer precisely separating religions or 'cultural identities', but still separating one world from another. The one, bruised and blemished by major violence, the pillages of poverty and dirty wars, is kept at a maximum distance by the other, which protects itself from it and justifies the distancing of this new 'impure' by fear of contamination. More insistent and complete than the politics of localized ghettos, but with the same inspiration as these, a great planetary segregation is born.

A world identified as dirty cannot but upset groups and nations that consider themselves clean. Thus when certain nations go to war, like the United States and NATO in Kosovo in 1999, they impose the dishonest notion of a 'clean war'. 'Full contact' is kept for the fiction of action films and video games. The absence of intervention on the ground, with concentration entirely on air strikes, attests to the hygienist desire for segregation, not to touch a dirty world.

By putting forward moral values that are literally embodied and transformed into palpable and natural manifestations, the justification of total rejection of the other by reference to their physical and moral blemishing by the war and violence that has touched them serves to keep this 'other' at the edge of the world and humanity, as ideally does the figure of the *pariah*, originally designating those 'untouchables' that Hindu society saw as outside of caste and impure, so that physical contact with them was symbolically polluting.

The biological and moral language, the invention of a bio-segregation, justify quarantine and at the end of the day the refusal of political dialogue as well as physical contact. 'Let them sort themselves out', and the blemished of today replace the savages of another time, but even more monstrous.

ONE WORLD REVEALS ANOTHER

For more than a year, from December 1999 to January 2001, hundreds of Colombian displaced persons occupied the offices of the International Red Cross in Bogotá, which they had invaded by force, in order to press their claims: long-term housing assistance, free education and health care, support for economic reintegration in the city. Though under continuous police surveillance, hundreds of adults and children, peasants, Indians, blacks and mestizos from all the regions ravaged by war, were filmed and interviewed by journalists and representatives of NGOs.

They established themselves within the four-storey building, but also occupied a portion of the street opposite the entrance to the Red Cross offices, in the very heart of the fashionable quarter of Bogotá, the *zona rosa*. This 'pink zone' is very busy by day with visitors to its clothing boutiques and brand-new shopping mall, and at night for its restaurants, cinemas and clubs.

After some months, a Bogotá newspaper described the bad smells that emanated from the encampment of *desplaza- dos* and had invaded the quarter. The hotels, restaurants and shops were losing their clients. The confrontation at the site of the occupation was a portrait in miniature of what was happening in the country as a whole, as another newspaper pointed out: 'Two Colombias that were formerly worlds apart are staring each other in the face day after day.'[16]

Can this kind of encounter lead to an awareness that there exists a common present? In the image of the confrontation created by an unexpected situation, in which two parts of humanity stared haggardly at one another for several months after never seeing one another before, can we still imagine that these worlds are going to cross, that a face-to-face encounter can take place in reality?

What remains today of the promises of this encounter? We see human masses parade on opaque televisions, their differ- ences being presented to us in very approximate terms, terms that at the end of the day are deceptive when they are sup- posed to explain who they are – 'Hutus', 'Tutsis', 'Moslems', 'guerrillas' – but terribly clear in the global common language of segregation: 'tribal wars', 'religious fundamentalisms', 'ancestral violence'. These notions are neither true nor false, they are simply incomplete and stigmatize those whom they name, in the image of those 'crumbs of thought' which Céline used in his *Journey to the End of Night* to depict the thinking of racist colonists in Africa in the early twentieth century.

These hasty and curtailed political commentaries serve to depict in summary form wars whose real stakes are not all mentioned, in particular the economic ones (diamonds, gold, petrol, water), their place in international political history being often sketched but their means remaining unknown: international arms traffic, drug networks, military training in the armies of the 'First World'. They describe these wars as other people's wars, other people's horrors, other people's exclusions, making out that if this warring world is the way it is, this is because it is ethnically different, and being so, does not concern us.

Let us then recall some recent memories of war in this 'First World' of Europe and North America: the popular support that Nazism received and the extermination of Jews, the mentally ill, homosexuals and Communists in the 1930s and 1940s, in a Germany and a Europe that today count among the leaders of the rich and 'clean' world; the half-century of disappearances, massacres and camps of Stalinism, the decision-making centre of which was located in the beautiful city of Moscow; the atrocities committed by French soldiers in the French colonies, particularly in Algeria in the 1950s; those of US soldiers in Vietnam during the 1960s.

It is possible to maintain then that no one has been spared by history, that all ethnic groups and cultures contain within them the possibility of extreme murderous violence. If this means little, it is not because the facts do not exist, but because the terms themselves – 'ethnic group', 'culture' – to which responsibility for violence is attributed are far too general and simplifying to explain the logical chain of actions leading to war or violence in a particular situation.

Thus, during the political violence in Brazzaville in 1997, one of the militias involved took the name of Nibolek. This term, now in the process of becoming a powerful ethnic category, is an acronym formed from the first syllables of three administrative and electoral territories, Niari, Bouenza and Lekemou, created a few years earlier in the south of the country.[17] While relating to a broader membership of the populations of southern Congo, it is clear enough that this identity does not immediately translate any precise differences in manners of living, thinking or speaking from other Congolese. It was born in the political difficulties of the democratization process begun by the National Sovereign Conference of 1991, and the quest for identity of the Brazzaville militias. Beliefs or affirmations of identity may play a mobilizing role in war at a particular moment, but this intervention, constructed in antagonism, exhorts and sometimes invents identities that confront other rival ones: in wars more than at any other time, these are identities with an external function. If in this context the reference to an essential, 'primordial' identity with apparent explanatory powers appears necessary, this remains a kind of 'virtual home' without 'real existence', as Claude Lévi-Strauss has remarked.[18]

These inventions and improvised constructions of identity are nothing new. The ethnic identities that are taken today as ancestral and have been frozen by history were often born under the sign of external partitions and descriptions, in many cases colonial ones. That ethnicity socially exists does not mean that it corresponds to a primal truth, pure and authentic. This explanatory 'truth' withers and weakens as soon as we restore the logic of events and processes, both ordinary and universal, that make certain identities exist or prevail in a given situation. Even when violence and war mobilize old ethnic or racial cleavages, such as those between Hutu and Tutsi in Rwanda, or Moors and Blacks in Mauretania, they arise out of unresolved political conflicts, distant and complex as these may be, from residues of the situation that often prolong such conflicts, and from the superposition of successive political crises. Then, in a society that finally no longer 'works', social breakdown and psychological disorder generate the possibility of extreme violence or 'senseless' wars.

Violence is not the expression of a conflict, but the opposite of conflict. It is what remains of a conflict that is denied, repressed, unfinished; it comes after politics, in the empty space that its disappearance leaves. Discourses of ethnic, racial or religious identity are also anchored in this empty space of politics, where violence has a place that is either already taken or there to be taken. Parties based on identity, if they facilitate the demand for a share of territory, for example, and are to that extent emancipatory, liberating people from a particular oppression and offering frameworks of protective defence with their own networks and hierarchies, still remain below the level of politics. This needs freedom for its existence; in Hannah Arendt's terms, politics needs a kind of freedom that is 'no longer tied physically or spiritually to a single position or point of view'.[19] It is only on this condition that politics can exist, with everything decided 'through words and persuasion, and not through force and violence'.[20]

The only proposal that is tenable, then, is to recreate the horizon of an ideal politics, seeking to restore an exclusive place to the political relationship between free human beings for governing their world. Many particular liberations, emancipation from multiple oppressions – racist, ethnonationalist or sexist –, are evidently needed before politics is appropriated by subjects with free judgement, unassigned to a discourse of identity. At the end of the day, however, this is the horizon that must be created. If so many regions, groups and countries today are touched by dirty war and violence, it is because in each case shared speech, accepted conflict and free politics have lost ground or have not succeeded in winning it. From this point of view, the bruised and 'dirty' worlds and the 'clean' countries still protected are embarked on the same history.

3

THE DESERT, THE CAMP, THE CITY

THE SPREADING DESERT

Hannah Arendt took up Nietzsche's formula, expressed in one of the *Zarathustra* poems, of concern about the 'spread of the desert', the disappearance of the intermediary space between people, which in her eyes constituted 'the world', in other words the totality of social relations from which politics is born.[1] 'The desert spreads': the desert is the opposite of the social and political exchange that unites all human beings, gathering them and distinguishing them at the same time.

The refugee camp is constructed, in its very principle, as an authentic 'desert', and not just because it is established in the hidden confines of Africa and Asia, far from the city. In itself, in the name of the welfare of victims and the effectiveness of interventions for their survival, it establishes an environment in which conversation and freedom are disturbing and troublesome. The common space between refugees, their 'world', is not desired or foreseen. In its place there is just an empty space, and so it remains, despite the recommencement of life that is attempted within it. The displaced, for their part, settle on the margins of cities; this is the same liminal quality that unites all situations of exodus, just as in the refugee camps. It is the very foundation of the camp as a place of waiting apart from society, and also the site of those displaced persons and refugees who have 'self-settled' in the sense that they dwell in peripheral zones of temporary or illegal occupation. Nothing can ever be totally achieved in such contexts, the incompleteness of the integration processes is cosubstantial to them, quarantine being their very horizon.

That is not all, for this desert replicates. Not only does it perpetuate itself in its particular place, but it extends to win space in international politics, reducing still more, on the planetary scale, the 'space-between-people'. The refugee camps are outside the place and time of the commonplace, ordinary and predictable world. They apply an exceptional regime, normally reserved for a margin, an edge of the world kept apart, just kept alive so it does not have to be thought, so that no overall consideration of it needs to be elaborated. But the world of ordinary humanity tends to retreat, too, as the spaces and situations that deny it continue to develop, the 'desert spreading' on all sides. The great planetary segregation does not protect anyone. It reduces still more the common space that constitutes the world. Those who live in a cosseted 'oasis', regarding a smooth image of the planet as a spectacle that does not affect them, have a momentary impression of protection. They have a clear strategy, honest enough, that aims to provide themselves and their loved ones with the resources needed, before confronting once again the deserts, the spaces without a 'world'.

This is why private cities, protected condominiums, gated communities, gain ground along with refugee camps, keeping the peripheries at a distance and voluntarily 'ghettoizing' themselves. They eliminate further parcels of the common space, other moments of exchange, to the point that people only exist now in their particular relationships, deprived of others and with no experience of differences. In this sense, we are directly touched by the spread of camps and margins, and share the fate of the refugees.

THE CAMPS: FROM EMERGENCY TO PERMANENCE

The ambition of refugee camps is to ensure the protection and survival of displaced persons even while war is still waging close at hand. Millions of refugees across the world live in these camps, in particular the 'sites' run by the UNHCR, varying in size from 2,000 (the camps for Mauretanians in Senegal) to 200,000 (the camps of Mugunga and Kibumba in the Goma region of former Zaïre). In Goma, several camps were located around a single base of humanitarian operations, forming a network that sheltered 750,000 people for more than two years, from 1994 to 1996: 'immense cities of huts in a desert of volcanic rock' came into being, as described in an account of the Rwandan refugees who lived there and gave a collective testimony of their experience.[2]

More rarely, camps house displaced persons within their own country, whether at the initiative of the UNHCR (though this is uncommon), or run by government services or various NGOs. Here again, these vary tremendously in size, running from a few hundred, such as the 'communities of peace' in Colombia, to more than 100,000, as in the camps for displaced persons from the southern Sudan, established under the government of that country in the environs of Khartoum.

This form of responsibility is clearly unstable, and depends on the further development of the conflicts in question. According to the geographer Luc Cambrezy, it is far more widespread in Africa and Asia, where it comprises respectively 83.2 per cent and 95.9 per cent of the refugees assisted by the UNHCR, whereas in Europe only 14.3 per cent of refugees live in such camps, others living in towns though benefiting from recognition as refugees and assistance from the UNHCR.[3]

Other projects formulated by the NGOs run in the same direction. This is the case for example with the 'zones of peace' established in the Philippines after 1998, spaces negotiated by international NGOs (supported by religious and traditional local authorities) with the armed groups, to keep fighting at a distance from established territories with precise borders, whether small or large. The same holds for the strategy of 'humanitarian spaces' developed by Médecins Sans Frontières from the late 1980s: a space is agreed in which freedom of dialogue with people who receive aid is guaranteed, freedom of movement and evaluation of the needs of the population, and freedom to verify the distribution of aid. The point is to shelter humanitarian intervention from the political and military pressure of warring groups, as Rony Brauman emphasizes.[4]

The establishment and development of refugee camps today is very diverse. In some cases, refugees are literally locked up in their camp, as the Kurds from Iraq were in Turkey between 1988 and 1992. In others, this is still the case in theory, but they manage to re-establish economic and other activities, as in Kenya or the former Zaïre. Others again are distributed among rural 'sites', like the 50,000 refugees, mainly Angolan, in the vast Maheba camp in Zambia, a portion of whom have been allocated agricultural land, even though they have to use illegal networks in order to sell their products. Villages populated by refugees exist in Uganda, also in the Mexican state of Chiapas, which has received Guatemalan refugees since the early 1980s.

The refugee camps have problems in maintaining their integrity, in other words ensuring the protection and neutrality of the spaces they comprise. They may become training camps for defeated armies, or depots for arms traffickers, but they can also suffer internal control by exiled ethnic or religious powers, the violent incursion of armies from their country of origin, or strategies of forced repatriation on the part of the national authorities.

The camps are often transformed into 'humanitarian sanctuaries':[5] in this case, refugees become targets or shields, even when the great majority of their inhabitants are civilians not involved in the conflict. Thus in 1996, in the camps of the Kivu region of the Democratic Republic of Congo (former Zaïre), Hutu refugees from Rwanda were exterminated by the forces of the 'Alliance' (Alliance of Democratic Forces for the Liberation of the Congo, directed by Laurent-Désiré Kabila), being viewed en bloc as responsible for the Rwandan genocide, even though three-quarters of them were women and children.[6]

The UNHCR has sought in various ways to ensure the protection of civilian populations in the midst of war: by 'zones of safety' aiming to protect the most fragile elements at particular points, that is, children, the elderly, pregnant women and sick people; 'neutralized zones', broader spaces defined within regions of combat and where the entire population, to the extent that it is not involved in the confrontations, is to be protected; finally, 'undefended localities', these being voluntarily disarmed and thus supposedly immune from attack.

All these situations of humanitarian emergency are legitimized only by being kept at a distance from war and politics. What happens to this legitimacy when the emergency is transformed into a lasting and permanent arrangement, and humanitarianism, based on exclusion from politics, is transformed into a situation of power, an instrument of political manipulation or an internationally accepted principle for governing the undesirables of the planet?

LIFE UNDER TRANSFUSION

These new and unforeseen situations are supposedly exceptional and temporary. Yet after a few months or years they become the everyday experience of thousands of people who are gathered in the same location and subject to the same authority, to rhythms and conditions of life that they have not chosen but were imposed on them as if they had fallen from another planet. If the refugees are grateful to these institutions for coming to their support, they are also forced to 'make do' and imagine their life in an unprecedented social context. The sense of living in a provisional situation never quite leaves their mind.

What is a refugee camp? It is an arrangement for policing, feeding and giving health care to a population that is offered refuge in order to shelter it from violent death arising from war or hunger. For the international sponsors of such camps, whether they are political such as the UNHCR or humanitarian such as the organizations of medical and social assistance, the camps incontestably represent the best emergency arrangement in operation: they make it possible to group people effectively, ensure protection and a minimal level of care for exiles who arrive en masse, hungry, destitute and often in very poor health.

A particularly instructive example is that of the three camps at Dadaab in north-eastern Kenya, which have existed since 1991–2 and seem unlikely to close in the near future. They have a similar population to the rest of the district of Garissa in which they are located (124,000 refugees in 2000), yet they do not appear on the map of the country. The Ifo camp (45,000 inhabitants and 10,000 shelters) was opened in September 1991, that of Dagahaley (34,000 inhabitants, around 7,000 shelters) in March 1992, and that of Hagadera (45,000 in habitants, 10,000 shelters) in June 1992. These camps are located at a distance of fifteen kilometres around. the village of Dadaab, where the international organizations that manage them have their headquarters. Their operation runs fairly well on the whole. The UNHCR exercises supreme power over the camps and coordinates humanitarian action.

'Security, food and health', say the responsible officials at Dadaab, or a minimal life under transfusion. The rations supplied by the UN's World Food Programme are distributed every two weeks by a Canadian NGO, Care, which stores the foodstuffs and allocates them with the help of a dozen or so representatives of refugees from different sectors or 'quarters' in each of the three camps.

Women line up, one at a time, in front of the distribution sheds, their UNHCR ration cards hanging from their neck or wrist: the card indicates the number of portions to which they are entitled. They emerge from the shed dragging behind them their sackful of supplies for the next two weeks. Further on, among the crowd of refugees who remain behind the protection barriers and entry gates defended with barbed wire, children and adolescents wait to carry the sacks to their huts. The fortnightly ration per head is made up of 6.75 kilos of maize (half of which can be replaced by wheat flour), 0.525 kilos of lentils, 0.375 litres of vegetable oil and 75 grams of salt. This set of foodstuffs, minutely counted, corresponds to about 1,900 calories per person per day, close to the norms of the UN's World Food Programme.

The health service is provided by the Belgian division of Médecins Sans Frontières. Each camp has three medical posts, as well as a mobile care team and a field hospital. This last is made up of a few sheds built of planks, with floors of cement or beaten earth; here and there, simple awnings have been attached to make covered spaces used as waiting rooms, consultation rooms or resting space. Babies and sick people are sleeping on mats. Everything is clean, and the medical staff, quite a number of them, are attentive and friendly. Nearly five hundred 'volunteers' (400 refugees and 100 from Dadaab village) work for MSF, divided between different sectors. The refugees who work for MSF or the other NGOs are considered to be 'volunteer community workers' inasmuch as they have no right to work on Kenyan territory. They do however receive a small monthly remuneration paid by the NGOs.

Malaria and TB are the two most widespread deadly infections. Malnutrition is monitored, and dealt with in a special room of the hospital. In general, this affects only 9 or 10 per cent of the population, particularly children between six months and three years. But the rate rises very rapidly when the supply of food aid, brought by lorry from the port of Mombasa, meets with difficulties or is interrupted because of bad weather. Following the floods caused in the region by the El Niño phenomenon from the end of 1997 through the early months of 1998, food was airlifted.

Security in the camp, finally, is effected by the Kenyan police under UNHCR supervision. A total of 250 men ensure order, supplied with uniforms and vehicles by the camp administration. On top of this, a UNHCR adviser (in fact, a US Vietnam veteran) trains and advises the police in protecting the camps against certain local problems: the rape of women in the surrounding bush when they go to collect wood for cooking, theft within the camp. In the centre of the small village of Dadaab, as at the entrance to each of the three sites, there is a police post. It is under police escort that the members of aid organizations and the UNHCR enter the refugee camps each morning and return at night, a twenty-minute journey. Towards 7:30 a.m., the procession arrives in the camps amid a cloud of dust left by their four-wheel drive vehicles, announcing the daily beginning of international assistance.

Among the dozen international organizations present in the Dadaab camps, the most significant, apart from the UNHCR itself, are Care (Canada), which supplies water, and stores and distributes food, Médecins Sans Frontières (Belgium) for health care, the German GTZ for wood supply, as well as the UN's World Food Programme and UNICEF for the construction and maintenance of wells. The Libyan NGO Al Haramein is responsible for teaching the Koran.

Visiting the camps rapidly gives rise to the conviction that an entire population is kept artificially alive by this international 'transfusion', and that any small dysfunction in the organization, due to weather conditions, local conflict, or a decision taken in New York, Geneva or Nairobi, could immediately compromise it or even reduce it to nothing. How can one be surprised that a culture of aid, made up of begging and dependence – what French writers have called *assistancialisme* – so rapidly permeates camp life, when aid is their only raison d'être and the sole authorized resource of the refugees?

OUTSIDE OF PLACE, OUTSIDE OF TIME

The camps remain in place for months if not years. Some close, others open, and sometimes refugees from a site that has been closed are transferred to another. If the conflicts in question are not resolved, social and economic conditions worsen in the country of origin and the exiles remain in their refuge. When peace is too fragile, some have the experience of repeated round trips between their country and the camp.

The agents of the UN and the relief organizations on the ground themselves recognize that they have no time to look at things from a long-term perspective, though they are themselves witness to this perpetuation and even its agents. Their intervention takes place in the name of an emergency, in which every action, every space, every establishment, is considered as temporary. But the precise duration of the 'emergency' is hard to determine. If no one is generally 'there' to intervene at the moment of a massacre, sacking or bombing, nor in the hours or days that follow it, everyone agrees that once camps have been established in a more or less rapid fashion, a certain inertia imposes itself – partly material, but especially administrative and logistic, and the situation persists for reasons that are internal as well as external. The continuation of war prevents the refugees' return to their homes, thus favouring their 'settlement' in the camps, and the aid system reinforces this by creating a market for employment. Across the world, more than 500 NGOs are working under contract from the UNHCR in order to intervene on the ground and organize all kinds of assistance. The members of these NGOs, just like some UN staff, may have a private interest in a camp's continuing in being, rather than its transformation. The refugees themselves see the aid organizations as a prized source of jobs and personal income, even if this remains tiny: their attachment is a function of the profound penury in which they live. But here again, all jobs are precarious, whether those of the NGO 'expats' (missions of six months, or a year at the most), those of the locals, or those of the 'volunteer' refugees. Everyone is supposed to see this work as a mission, a contract or an opportunity not to be renewed. Precariousness is official, and not just a function of circumstances as is generally supposed.

At all levels, therefore, humanitarian intervention has a tendency, along with the emergency practice, to become

frozen and fixed at the sites of its implantation. Yet the difficulty of giving a sense to these social artefacts equally affects
the great mass of 'inhabitants'. As if the experience of displacement and refuge were not just outside all social systems,
but also outside any social thought: the 'before' (war, violence) and the 'after' (peace, return or resettlement) are the
subject of many commentaries and political discussions, but
the 'during' is not: it is a present whose duration is unthinkable. To speak of the time spent in the camps is a disturbing
subject: durable life is not supposed to exist in a space outside
of place, a moment outside of time, an identity without community, and in this respect it is upsetting and unnameable.

The only status acceptable in the camps, and even decreed,
is that of victim. The refugees are in a state of waiting, they
generally have no right to work the land on which they find
themselves, nor to take any kind of employment, since life is
'given' them by the humanitarian principle. The application
of this principle establishes a contradiction between minimal
biological life (protection, feeding, health) and the social and
political existence of individuals: the refugees are certainly
alive, but they no longer 'exist'. According to the humanitarian – and in a certain sense, humanist – principle that concerns itself with mere survival, whatever might be the
individual's nationality, ethnicity or religion, and their past in
the war, this social identity is now put in brackets for as long
as they are confined to the transit zone. Having already lost
the mediations that founded their social existence, in other
words an ordinary set of things and people with an established meaning – land, home, village, town, relatives, goods,
work and other everyday bearings – these wandering and
waiting beings no longer have anything but their 'bare lives',
the maintenance of which depends on humanitarian aid.

They spend months and years, sometimes entire life-cycles
– the whole of childhood, adolescence, or old age – outside of

any institutional tie. Thus in Kenya, a refugee has no identity of any kind, anywhere. He or she has no national or international card corresponding to their present situation, which they could show in return for the right to move around and live in society. The only administrative document that the refugees possess is the ration card of the World Food Programme, or literally a right to remain alive within the strict limits of the camp. Hanging from the neck or the wrist, this ration card might seem a humiliating document. But it is the sole title that ties these refugees to the world of institutions, and in general the only official symbol of recognition for the individual who possesses it. It is accordingly prized, and the object of different kinds of trafficking: resale, inflation of the number of beneficiaries, attribution to 'false' refugees, etc. A strange situation that faces the refugees with the only choice of action that between passive accommodation to outside assistance, and illegality.

A MUSEUM OF DIFFERENCES WITH THE AIR OF A SHANTY-TOWN

At the beginning, it all seemed quite straightforward. Emergencies raised only technical operational problems. Then the social complexity of the camps began to emerge, day after day. We can follow the steps of the refugees in their camp, from the time they settle there, get their bearings and organize themselves in space, and see how the humanitarian mechanism for their survival becomes for them a network of relationships within which a semblance of social hierarchy arises. How in due course, the empty space begins to fill and take life, and how a kind of town takes shape without ever having been envisaged.

In Kenya, the UNHCR started by constructing fences made up of stakes and barbed wire for several kilometres

around the Dadaab camps as an external boundary, and likewise dividing them internally into plots of some two to three
hectares each, in which the refugees were grouped according
to their place of departure, ethnic group or in some cases
original clan. Each of these 'blocks', as they came to be
called, contained 100 shelters to house around 500 refugees,
their limits being cordoned off to permit the passage of
police and medical vehicles, or construction materials.

On their arrival, they all received the same blue-and-white
plastic sheet from the UNHCR, a mattress, and some cooking utensils. They went out to find wood around the camp to
construct shelters. As the years went by, they tried to construct replicas of their old homes, but with the means at
hand and in a different setting. Thus they gradually formed
the image of an immense ethnographic museum which tried
to resist transformation into a mere shanty-town.

In this museum, the camps exhibit different features that
are grouped together outside of their original context. The
circular huts made of branches, covered with a couple of
pieces of UNHCR plastic sheeting, form the most widespread habitat in the Dadaab camps, and house principally
ethnic Soomaalis, rural and nomadic, as well as a number of
townspeople who have had their shelters built by those with
the requisite know-how. For some urban Soomaalis, and
those known as 'Bantu Soomaalis',[7] these are rectangular huts
of mud and half-timber covered with metal sheeting, thatch,
or plastic sheets serving as roofs, walls or awnings. Tiles,
doors and sometimes shutters, low tables and chicken coops
are constructed with boxes and sheeting made from the big
tins of oil and lentils of the World Food Programme, bearing
the stamp of the humanitarian donors: 'USA', 'EEC', 'Japan',
'WFP', 'UNHCR', so that these respective flags dot the
landscape. It is these above all that give this museum a different air from that of a shanty-town – a world of improvisation

and residue, a new context for this strange ethnographic exhibition.

Some anonymous spaces have been given names by the refugees. Hagadera, one of the three Dadaab sites, is divided into two major sets of shelters that have come to be known in the Soomaali language as *baat wein* (sandy ground) and *gadwday* (red sand), as a function of the different kind of soil. But above all it is the space of the market, located at the entrance to the first 'quarter' of the camp, that attracts attention. Here, the refugees and some local people make their exchanges along two sand strips bordered with stalls selling food rations and other basic necessities, as well as serving coffee and offering video screenings, in shelters known respectively as 'coffee shops' and 'video shops'. This lively place supplied with electricity from generators, where a bit of commerce is found, as well as some non-refugees, where you can watch the arrival and departure of buses or the vehicles of the aid organizations, is the place that the refugees have chosen to call their 'town' (*magalo* in Soomaali). In the same fashion, the street passing close to the market is called by the English name of 'main street'. The stretch of sand (50 metres wide, a kilometre long) that the refugees traverse, on foot and often under a torrid sun, to go from the entrance and the market to their shelters, is called, also in English, the 'highway'.

These little reinventions of everyday life in the camps are comparable to those which, according to Michel de Certeau,[8] mark the resistance of townspeople to the individualization and anonymity of urban space. Here at Dadaab, children play ball on wide unmarked ground, and learn to communicate in a number of languages. Women give birth (4,000 each year) in the precarious field hospitals established in the camps. Marriages are celebrated in Catholic or Orthodox churches, as well as in mosques, all these religious buildings being made of earth, plastic sheets, and whatever material is at hand. The stalls display part of the food rations as well as other provisions that are in short supply (onions, tomatoes, meat, milk) and individual cigarettes. Day after day, a bit of life grows up on the soil of these strange towns planted in the midst of a bare and arid bush, scorched by the dry and dusty air of the burning winds.

LIFE WITHOUT SOCIETY

Here and there hybrid and embryonic forms of social differentiation grow up. Attempted towns transform the space on which the camps are built: these gradually become places where a social and economic life is reinvented, with power relations that are non-existent elsewhere.

The background, however, is the inactivity that dominates camp life. This problem is a corollary of the sense of abandonment and affects everyone, though most directly those who before the exodus had a recognized job – a minor civil servant or waged worker, thus urban men in particular. Moral suffering, even psychological troubles bound up with professional inactivity, occupy an important place. Somalians previously employed in commerce, services or administration in Mogadishu no longer know what to do; young people seek ways of 'pushing time' in their block; former Ethiopian civil servants, after nine years of exile and camp life, view themselves as 'physically and mentally imprisoned, homeless and hopeless' and talk of suicide. In a repetitive way, the refugees express above all feelings of impotence and uselessness.

There is no official labour market in the camps, and since they are seen as foreigners and have no work permits, 'those working outside the camps are illegal', as a UNHCR official emphasizes. Yet some business is more or less recognized or tolerated, and is visible from a tour round the camps: resale of part of the food ration, and also on the market stalls the trade in basic necessities brought from Garissa, the district capital; raising of goats in the area around the camps, small-scale handicrafts in and around the huts and cabins (basket-weaving, sewing, carpentry, metalwork, tailoring, building); coffee and tea shops, hairdressing, and other services.

A certain capital, networks and institutions are needed for this embryonic economy to turn. Soomaali traders and herdsmen play an important role. For the members of the Ogaden clan, the largest group, the Dadaab camps are eco-logically and culturally continuous with their own, located just the other side of the Somalian frontier. They circulate easily in the region, and sometimes their hosts, villagers or townspeople, are able to help them acquire financial auton-omy (work, a loan, etc.).[9]

A Kenyan identity card or driving licence, or a temporary work card that is regularly renewed, can be obtained for a fee with the complicity of officials charged with issuing or controlling documents outside the camps, and enable their holders to conduct some kind of business. These activities can lead to people establishing themselves clandestinely in Garissa or in the suburbs of Nairobi, even making return trips to Somalia. Some refugees living in the camps regularly receive assistance from brothers or sons who move around the country and work without declaring themselves either as foreigners or refugees. Both categories also receive financial support from abroad, sent by relatives who have sought refugee in other countries (Europe, Canada, United States, etc.), as well as those living in Somalia or other parts of Kenya. These financial operations are conducted in parallel banks, thanks to trusted contacts in the places where the funds originate. This money enables refugees to supplement the World Food Programme ration, as well as to launch themselves in small-scale trade in the camp markets.

Commercial and handicraft activity is also supported by international NGOs, as it provides a way of combating the refugees' inactivity, and above all has an educational or social value. In effect, this support is conceived as socially upgrading certain categories viewed as 'vulnerable': young orphans, the physically handicapped, women who have been widowed, divorced or raped.

The same assistance is also offered to minority groups who are discriminated against in the context of the camp, for example, Soomaali castes and clans considered inferior and servile. By way of loans of 5,000 Kenyan shillings (about 75 euros / $100), sometimes more, some 250 groups of four or five people had managed to develop, by June 2000, projects known as 'income-generating activities'. In fact, any strictly economic profitability is accidental, and does not seem to be the main purpose of the funding bodies. Thus the products of women's basket-weaving are sold at a derisory price (50 to 100 shillings depending on size, or the price of a bus ticket from one camp to the other), yet unsold baskets pile up in the huts of the women who produce them. Only welfare initiatives make it possible to sell some on a wholesale basis, for example on the occasion of official visits to the camps by ambassadors or UN representatives. Everything happens as if from the point of view of the funders as well as their beneficiaries, what matters is to maintain an appearance of economic activity, in which regular work is tangible proof of a continuing social utility.

Finally, the NGOs involved in the camps employ and pay a total of 1,500 refugees in the three sites as 'volunteer community workers' (400 employed by MSF, 600 by Care, others by the UNHCR, the World Food Programme, the German agency for technical cooperation GTZ, etc.) These receive wages – unofficially, since under Kenyan legislation they have no right to work; their pay ranges from 2,500 to 4,000 Kenyan shillings per month (38 to 60 euros / $50–$80). This income enables them to complement their food ration, but not just this. It helps them pay others to construct dwellings of better quality than the UNCHR tents, employ others to work for them (cooking, maintenance), invest in small business (sale of vegetables on the market stalls) or assist the operation of certain lucrative services (photo studio or video shop) run by friends, for example by copying onto video cassettes international sporting events that are transmitted direct, via satellite, to television sets in the compound of the relief organizations; these are then hired out the next day at the video shops.

These little activities and resources show a social differentiation specific to the camps. At the top of the status hierarchy are a small minority of Soomaali notables, composed of traders, herders, and chiefs of those clans with a superior status. The 'volunteer community workers', for their part, represent an alternative minority, close enough to the former as regards their number and income, but competing with them in ideological terms. The grouping formed by the petty traders, occasional handicraft workers and informal employees makes up a third, heterogeneous category, dependent on the two higher strata, but also on the support of the NGOs. A fourth and final level is constituted by those who have nothing and do nothing, simply benefiting from the minimum level of relief: food, health care, water, firewood, and shelter, possibly complemented by occasional aid from the other categories mentioned above, or from relatives living outside the camps. This is by far the most numerous category (some two-thirds of the total population);[10] it reminds us that the common and permanent basis of the life of the camps is marked by destitution and inactivity; the rest only appears in contrast against this.

These social categories, in particular the Soomaali notables and traders, the volunteer community workers, and the handicraft workers and salespeople (dependent or subsidized), give the impression that this space could be described like any other social microcosm. It shows forms of social classes that could acquire a full reality and effectiveness if it were possible to link them into an overall and determining framework, even one invisible on the ground: a history, a society, an economy and institutions of which the camp's social hierarchy would be the actual localized embodiment. But this is in no way the case. Each category has its distinct origins, and the overall stratification is based on fragmented social logics: the logic of clans and the logic of humanitarianism, the UN policy and Soomaali ethno-nationalism, therapeutic work and informal economy; the living space of the camps does not 'represent' any existing society, rather fragments of societies whose common point is that their recent history has met with war on its path. More certainly, it represents one of the many manifestations of cultural and social hybridization that characterize our planet as a global whole.

BARE TOWNS

An economy that would be able to exist, as people demonstrate their readiness to work; an occupation of space that, precarious as it is, defines its environment as somewhere between the model of urban peripheries – the Asian slum or Latin American '*invasión*' – and that of an African village that has grown to gigantic size; a world of relationships operating by way of proximities, conflicts, alliances, intersection of collective strategies and individual choices; political actions addressed to interlocutors from several worlds previously unconnected . . . Everyone who has observed the refugee camps can see there a kind of town, not just in terms of size, but by the forms of life that seem to seek new expression.

The camp is comparable to a town, but this status is unachieved. Everything is potential but nothing develops, no promise of life is really fulfilled. Conflicts are stopped by means of forced repatriation or removal to another camp. Any kind of work remains illegal, even if tolerated up to a certain point, and the few handicraft products that are made (like the famous wicker baskets) find no consumer market, or hardly any. Only the 'video shops' are always full, showing Indian or American films and international sporting events; the benches are overcrowded, people look over their neighbour's shoulder to see the tiny television at the back of the hut: a little window on the other world, at least.

The refugee camps often have a rectilinear plan, those of Dadaab not excluded. This is nothing new, it dates from the ancient Greek pattern and inspired colonial town-planning in Latin America and Africa. It shows that the agglomeration of people at a particular place was conceived before it was realized. As seats of European power, the colonial towns were also built to concentrate an indigenous population, often in separate districts, to make them work in the context of the capitalist colonial system. Gradually a division of labour and political systems were established; social categories and indigenous political groups were formed, which overthrew or outgrew the colonial structures. In the camps, however, neither work (as economic activity) nor politics (as autonomous action) is able to develop and consolidate itself. The camps remain bare towns like the indigenous quarters of colonial towns that history might have frozen in time.

The camps are thus more comparable to the 'townships' of apartheid South Africa, set up under the Group Areas Act of 1950, which officially imposed racial separation of habitation zones until the early 1990s. 'Townships' were urban forms amputated of an entire part of life, that of economics, politics, and the encounter with higher social classes (and whites). But the township residents travelled out each day to work in the mines and cities where they had jobs and met white people. And the means of transport indispensable to the operation of apartheid (trains in particular) often became sites of contestation and political organization against apartheid. Refugee camps, for their part, while amputated in a similar way, have no compensation for this amputation.

The camps thus form an urban reality marked both by the frozen time of the indigenous quarters of colonial towns, and by the amputation of apartheid townships. While certain ideologists of institutional racism hailed the 'separate development' of those they kept at a distance, today people like to speak in international circles of 'sustainable development' in the countries of the South, but what the displaced people and refugees experience for their part is a reality of a quite new type: a lasting and separate non-development.

PLANETARY SEGREGATION

New urban models are being prepared. At the opposite extreme from the countries of refugees, but still on the same planet, the rich multiply their 'gated communities', in which people deliberately group themselves on a basis of resemblance and affinity: closed communities of over-55s or golf addicts, private suburbs for identical families of the same socio-professional type, higher income level or lifestyle preference.[11] Shut up in communities circled by walls and barbed wire, they protect themselves by means of private police forces, preventing any physical expression of difference. So similar on the inside, from the outside they appear a gathering of the arrogant and privileged.

The refugee camps, on the other hand, are 'gated identities' walled in from outside: ethnic, racial, and national identities that have been bruised by war, massacre and flight, but beyond this and more generally, identities of survivors suspected of being guilty, accomplices, diseased or marked by dirty wars. One is the mirror image of the other, with the stigmata being copied. Wars and barbed wire, gates and police, are present on both sides.

Gated communities facing gated identities: the co-presence of these two closed worlds expresses a new urban eugenics, an elementary system of bio-segregation anterior to any thought of the other, compatible only with thinking of oneself, to the point of self-obsession and fear of the least physical contact. In the same phenomenon of rejection, the homeless, young vagrants, those displaced by hunger, and those suffering from AIDS, join with refugees in the world of gated identities. In the Dadaab camps, TB patients who find no one to care for them on their home ground arrive spontaneously from a long way away to get treatment at the MSF hospitals; they try and pass as refugees, but without a food ration card they are reduced to begging at the market, sleeping in the mosques made of wooden boards and plastic sheets, and become refugees even among the refugees.

The geopolitical use of the camps and of humanitarian aid is already a reality evidenced in many situations. The breach thus opened may widen tomorrow, engulfing a large share of humanity, but one set apart from the rest of the world and thus neglectable if not negligible. Might humanitarians then find themselves acting as low-cost managers of exclusion on a planetary scale, without this being any longer a matter of emergency, accident or exceptional circumstances? It is even possible that, at the same time, any sense of bad conscience towards the condemned part of humanity would be lost: all that is needed for this is that the movement of bio-segregation already under way should continue, creating and freezing the identities sullied by war, violence and exodus, as well as by disease, poverty and illegality. The 'bearers' of these stigmata could be kept decisively at a distance in the name of their lesser humanity, even a dehumanization that is both physical and moral.

The refugee camps of today are the most advanced form of a global treatment of stigmatized identities and undesirable groups. And at the same time, they are laboratories in which still unconceived forms of urbanism are germinating.

A DETESTABLE LIMINALITY

It was inevitable, but it is disturbing. The paradox of humanitarian aid can be summed up in this single sentence: the humanitarian intention is not questionable as such, as an emergency solution whose necessity is highlighted by each new drama, the search for a response that is quickest and best adapted to the sufferings of individuals. Yet its effects are completely in conformity with this extreme modernity in which all kinds of social disaffiliation multiply, with their loss of identity and withdrawal, phenomena that Marc Augé has identified as the consequences of an over-modernity, a modernity pressed to excess, which seems to spread today to every latitude.[12] Let us examine this paradox more closely, and propose some theoretical markers with a view to imagining its possible extensions.

The refugee camps establish a kind of social quarantine in the face of humanitarian and geopolitical risks. Their enclosure makes refugees into beings still less than those 'useless souls' taken in by the hospices of the Middle Ages. Though 'useless', they were none the less present at the heart of the city: crippled, sick, old people and other unfortunates, even those who faked destitution and illness, could find assistance at the 'shelter of the ramparts' of medieval Paris.[13] Only lepers were located outside the city wall, but at no great distance.[14]

The situation with refugees today is quite the opposite. The compassion of some people, the fear or hatred of others, produce the same distancing effect. As soon as the emergency is past, the humanitarian moment in the strict sense, refugees appear as an awkward encumbrance. They are at the end of the day undesirable, kept apart from the world, far from the city. Living an indefinite life, 'separated from its context, and which, having as it were survived death, has become incompatible with the human world' – these are the terms in which the philosopher Giorgio Agamben describes their 'bare life'[15] – refugees are kept in quarantine as a function of the political inability to conceive their place in society as a whole. Set down in a desert of stone or sand, in dry bush or other uninhabited or empty space, they are the very figure of a detestable liminality.

This abandonment of 'useless' people and regions has developed at the level of world economics and politics, and we should recall that the form of the camps can very well serve strategies of separation, either temporary or permanent. Humanitarianism then becomes a second-best to integration for all those who, for various reasons, we do not want to integrate into the social and political world of human beings, keeping them instead in vague waiting-rooms, *on the margins of the world*. Beyond the function of the camps for emergency rescue, they are inscribed in this broader perspective: formation of a global space of humanitarian management of those of the planet's population who are most unwanted and undesirable.

The established powers of the refugee camps are the UN and humanitarian organizations that ensure the good operation of the systems of policing, food supply and medical care. Their attitude is based on the necessary belief that they are faced with beings who are neither friends nor enemies, neither fellow-citizens nor foreigners; beings who are a priori

unnameable, who arrive in the camp only as victims, naked
and suffering, 'pure life without any mediation'.[16] In a certain sense, the camp *makes the empty space* around these lives
that are bared and placed under the dependence of global
humanitarianism because of violence, war and exodus. Does
the camp then form, as Agamben's studies suggest, a 'bio-
political' paradigm, in the sense that the camp powers establish the ultimate and essential form of a 'politics of living
beings' as the model of a possible politics for society as a
whole, logical and irrefutable despite its frightening character? Or is it rather the opposite, a model of 'non-politics', i.e.
a pure mechanism of bio-*power*, thus leaving a margin or
breach in which subjects by their action can appropriate
politics?[17] It is only possible to assimilate bio-power and bio-
politics if one 'avoids the question of political subjectification'.[18] This is the question that interests us here, up to the
limits of the incompatibility between absolute power over
life and the concrete forms of political subjectification. Let
us dwell for a moment on the relationships between power,
police and politics, since these closely concern the life of the
refugees.

The regular and everyday operation of the camps depends
essentially on the presence of a *police*. In principle security is
controlled by the UNHCR (whether through national
armies, the UNHCR's own services, or UN forces), despite a
number of possible kinds of disorder that we have already
mentioned (external or internal attacks, arms trading, internal action of armed groups, and so on). This order exists so
as to ensure the immediate power of international organizations over the very lives of the individuals grouped in the
camps. It is compatible with a notion of humanitarian aid,
to the extent that the efficacy of this implies a policing
order devoid of mediation. Democratic 'conversation', on
the contrary, would considerably obstruct it at moments of

emergency and insecurity, when life itself is at stake. In emergency situations all that matters is victims, and victims, in humanitarian thinking, have no social or political affiliation, and thus no voice.

The globally shared conviction that 'it's for their own good' sees refugee camps as the very opposite to prison camps or concentration camps. And yet they too establish a framework of organization and command that is incompatible with politics – in the sense of speech shared between equals living within the *polis*, 'the most talkative of all bodies politic'.[19]

What we have here is not a relationship that would unify the essence of the political with its appearance (the camp is not a political form in itself), but rather an alternative between on the one hand a situation of power carried to excess, which obstructs any political space based on shared speech, and on the other hand a world of relationships that tends on the contrary to recreate this. This hypothesis, which we shall return to later, valorizes the ambivalence of the camps and makes it possible to investigate the formation of political systems within them. The subject we are speaking of here can be for the ethnologist what the agent is to the sociologist and the citizen to the political scientist. We have already observed such subjects in the urban peripheries, when leaders arise from a social milieu that 'carries' them as much as being represented by them.[20] The subjectification of politics that is accomplished here is translated at the end of the day into the reconquest of an identity and control of each person over their destiny. The space of the refugee camp is thus traversed by a fundamental tension between the voiceless humanitarian victim and the subject that begins forming again as soon as a context of socialization is reborn and brings about the existence of public spaces, exchange, projects for individual and collective life. But the strangeness of this context is not without consequence on the detours of this subjectification.

In practical and political terms, the existence of speech and the formation of subjects is a key question for the hypothesis of a 'community' of displaced persons and refugees. In the context of the denial of politics that the organization of the refugee camp represents in principle (a denial based both on humanitarian principle and on the situation of 'power over life'), subjectification can only take paths that are novel from the perspective of political tradition. It is born from social eruptions, unforeseen events and actions (organizational, reclamatory or protest) that are waged at the heart of spaces of forced inaction.

All these forms of initiative and speech make conceivable a transition from the camp to the city, in the sense of the *polis* as well as that of urban sociability. By virtue of their very heterogeneity, the camps can become the origin of unplanned towns, new contexts for socialization, relationships and identification. Though we may already glimpse their supersession, at the same time the order of emergencies or geopolitical imperatives obstructs the achievement of this transformation. The town is in the camp, but only in the form of attempts that are constantly aborted. This ambivalence and tension translates into a reality that is ambiguous, undetermined and unfulfilled: the camp-towns are neither completely closed nor completely open, refugees are neither completely dead as subject, nor completely alive.

REFUGEES, 'BIG MEN' AND OURSELVES

In February 2002 a report of the Save the Children Fund on 'Sexual Violence and Exploitation: The Experience of Refugee Children in Guinea, Liberia and Sierra Leone' found an unexpected audience in the European public – after the text, not originally designed to be made public, had been widely circulated on the internet. As an exemplary case of a scandalous revelation of the world of refugees and humanitarian aid, the facts described in this report (and confusedly repeated from one media to another) were the object of a unanimous moral condemnation that was both flashy and fleeting.

The individuals discussed in the Save the Children report are 'children' in the sense of the 1989 UN convention on the Rights of the Child, that is, less than eighteen years of age. Transition to adult life, however, often occurs rather younger, both in Africa and elsewhere: independent work and habitat for 'street children', marriage or pre-marital motherhood for girls of all social classes from the start of adolescence, and not just for refugees. In the camps described by the STC report, the great majority of victims were girls aged between thirteen and eighteen. Acts of paedophilia or outright rape, with physical threats and violence, are mentioned only exceptionally in this report, though not completely absent. What is involved in a very general sense is 'sexual exploitation', an elementary and organized form of prostitution: the direct exchange of sexual favours for a bit of food, a plastic sheet, a blanket, a bar of soap, or possibly a small sum of money.

A rigid moral condemnation of sexual faults is thus ineffective: it only bears on a tiny portion of the facts recounted, and says nothing about the social milieu that generates these. Moreover, these facts were described on the basis of indirect evidence, without suspects, victims or direct witnesses being personally indicated. A few months after revelations that the media were quick to describe as 'sexual scandals', 'humanitarian rape' or 'sordid humanitarianism', the affair was ended by an acquittal for want of tangible proof of criminal offences. The UN's office for internal control published a report in October 2002 that left the matter vague: there had indeed been sexual abuses, which might possibly have involved aid workers, but there had been nothing systematic, although the problem was 'genuine'. Etcetera. In the wake of these events some NGOs tried to define more specifically what was meant by 'abuse of power', and to draw up codes of conduct for their agents.

But the facts described in the evidence on which the Save the Children report was based are all too sadly common-place in their context to be assimilated to a general and undifferentiated presence of perversion, debauchery and other sexual harassment on which the press so eagerly seizes, whether in France, Europe or America. The involve-ment of 'international agents' (that is, whites) from NGOs or UN bodies in such sexual abuse of under-age refugees was mentioned unofficially, but does not appear in the writ-ten report. The question is an important one from the standpoint of the white post-colonial conscience; what pre-occupies 'us' is whether this is more or less clean or dirty. On the other hand, if it is proved that Western agents really were involved, that is only one form of abjection among others produced by a general state of social distress and impunity. It is this general state that we should be dis-cussing more seriously.

The 'sexual exploiters' of under-age refugees are essen-tially adult men belonging to those social categories that have some form of power in the camps. If so much attention has been paid to the mention in the Save the Children report of certain NGO and UN agents (workers of national or local origin, and refugees employed by the NGOs), other cate-gories have been equally represented among the agents of sexual abuse: police and soldiers of national armies, regional units of the UN peace-keeping forces, teachers (nationals or refugees) in schools run by governments or NGOs, refugee representatives (community or religious leaders), refugees with commercial activities in the camps, and ultimately any man in the region with some kind of job, income, and access to the camps (traders, diamond miners, plantation workers, depending on the situation). We have here the set of categories that habitually occupy 'superior' positions in the social world of the refugee camps: the minors who gave evidence to the Save the Children enquiry refer to them as 'big men'.

The camps are social microcosms that seem almost ordinary, despite their hybrid and artificial formation. As well as terrible destitution they also display the beginnings of social hierarchy, attempts at an informal economy, prostitution, various kinds of churches, etc. They are in some cases 'camp-towns', immense conurbations that pretend to be provisional. Their difference, and what makes possible all these abuses, is based on the deterioration of social life in and through war, which feeds them with new arrivals, and on the existence of an exceptional regime that governs the lives of refugees parked there so far from our view.

In these camps, as elsewhere, prostitution and sexual abuse against minors flourish, due not only to material deprivation, but also to the disappearance or dislocation of the social environment for the great majority of refugees. The loss of parents and relatives killed at their place of origin or along the refugees' itinerary, the dispersal of families in flight, hunger and disease, all these factors affect refugees indiscriminately and diminish them both physically and socially – especially women and children, who are often isolated survivors of massacres. This vulnerability gives still more strength to the absolute power possessed in the camps by anyone having a bit of money or food. In this case there is neither 'rape' or harassment, nor even explicit pressure. The very context makes criminal action unnecessary for the 'big man'.

Established as emergency solutions, the camps gradually come to represent the context of everyday life for their 'inhabitants' over long years, sometimes even decades. Lacking any control over the time they pass there or the policies applied, the refugees then find themselves for the duration in an exceptional space. Having no right to circulate or work in the countries where the UNHCR sites are located, those who leave the camps do so by special and temporary permission, or else clandestinely. They have no actual citizenship (neither that of the country they left, nor that of the country receiving them), and the only 'right' they have is that granted by those individuals who have power here over their lives. This exceptional situation can act for the worse, but it can also have beneficial effects: sometimes humanitarian organizations develop programmes of female health awareness, against sexual abuse and rape in and around the camps, or against violence within the family; they carry out peace education programmes, establish post-traumatic talk groups, and so on. But this does not prevent that fact that in one camp or another, or in one part of a camp, other individuals may not lay down their own rules. And this has the most weight in the life of the camps.

In a refugee camp in an African country that could well have been part of the Save the Children investigation, the UNHCR had delegated its powers to the national branch of a major international religious NGO. This body employed nationals of the country in question as agents, both locals and refugees; they were used to working in the camp and moving in due course from one NGO to another. One of these was specifically in charge of transit centres; he was a refugee himself, who had arrived at the camp more than twenty years ago. The transit centres are sites where new refugees arrive from the border, tired, hungry and often ill. They represent an end point in the humanitarian chain, a critical place for checking its effectiveness, but are equally a 'terrain' where this man is the sole official from the NGO to visit regularly. In the transit centre, moving between the tents, the NGO representative distributes tiny amounts of soap to some, cooking utensils to others, and in a few cases blankets; it takes anything from two days to a week for food to be distributed to new refugees. The NGO agent knocks some people down, insults others, calls one person a liar and another a thief, simply because she asks for a plastic sheet which he says he gave her yesterday. The same man is in charge of the allocation of sites on which to plant four posts and a cover marked UNHCR, and he distributes, divides, groups or separates the refugees by pointing a finger and screaming at those who complain. These have been in the transit tents for a month, and he seems to know them well. He threatens a youth whom he suspects of being a robber, kisses a young woman, is hugged by a young man, enters and remains in the tents as he pleases. If this is the particular moment of the abuse of power, including sexual abuse, it is inscribed in a deep social wretchedness combined with a political exceptionalism, a situation of 'power over life'. The UNHCR delegates to the NGO, which delegates to this one man 'on the ground' who lays down the law as he pleases. . . and thus practises one of the forms of a general regime of exceptionalism.

The refugee camps are not exactly zones without law, rather zones with exceptional rights and powers, in which everything is possible for those in control. In the same camp, several volunteers from international NGOs, including Médecins Sans Frontières and the Jesuit Relief Service, protested to the UNHCR about administrative dysfunction. Five employees from the camp administration had been unofficially recognized as embezzling food and funds and practising sexual abuse, including the person directly responsible for distributing food to the 25,000 refugees on the site. Although no legal charge had been brought against them, they were dismissed from their functions and had to leave the camp. As for the 'man on the ground' mentioned above, he resigned and left in a hurry, but not before having delivered a written denunciation of the many practices of embezzling money and material that he had observed within the NGO that administered the camp employing him.

These humanitarian (or military-humanitarian) spaces, like the Australian system of detention camps, are kept at a distance from the places of ordinary life. We look at them from the basis of an ego-centred relationship of the centre-periphery type; this view is interested in the details of internal life at the human periphery only to the extent that they question the centre itself. Thus the 'scandal' of sexual abuse of under-age refugees suddenly vanishes as soon as the innocence of the whites has been asserted. Our morality is saved, the operation, perversion and corruption of humanitarian sites can be classed as an 'exception', an extra-territoriality in which arbitrary actions and those responsible for them act freely in their own 'order of things'. In the best case, a balance of forces is established within the camps that permits modes of authority to be defined in a more open manner. The introduction of 'disorder', actions and words that are unforeseen and dissonant in these spaces, is finally the best outcome in the circumstances. The emergence of this disorder in the world created by war and forced displacement, the distancing of undesirables and humanitarian action, are the subject to which we must finally bear our attention.

While moral denunciation from a distance maintains above all a stigmatizing at the expense of the refugees themselves, a critical attention that focuses within these worlds of refugees, those internally displaced and those in camps, is the basis for a political critique, and one that is far more radical. What on reflection proves genuinely useful is not just to denounce one more scandal (sexual, moral, financial) from a distance and simply cleanse our own conscience, given that these 'scandals' are simply part and parcel of everyday life in these spaces. It is rather to resist by all means possible the establishment on a global scale of a regime of exceptionalism – in camps, on islands, in port zones – that is of interminable delay, as well as other forms of quarantine in which so many millions of undesirables are confined.[21]

THE RIGHT TO LIFE

EXISTENTIAL COMMUNITIES

The population is a heterogeneous one: in terms of the particular conditions of its exodus, its wait in the camps or on the edges of towns, as likewise in terms of the legal status of the displaced person, refugee, or illegal immigrant. Equally heterogeneous are the causes of the warfare and violence at the origin of these departures, as well as the nationalities, ethnic and religious groups involved. Yet a more essential unity constitutes this population as a world apart, and one that is relatively unified: an identity of existence that is unforeseen, unnameable, and on the margins of common humanity.[1] In war and exodus, the 'minimum identity' of each victim is in danger, that which lies at the basis of the unity of the human, and makes the most varied experiences 'mutually comprehensible, at least to a degree'.[2]

This impassable universalism of identity is put in question by the experience of dirty war, massacre, sudden loss of the several sociological foundations of identity (place, belongings, work, relatives and friends), which have to be rebuilt one by one for the lost humanity to be regained in action.

The three moments of destruction, confinement, and action for the right to life constitute the world of refugees and displaced people into a whole, different from any other. They found a kind of community of exodus, which is neither ethnic nor religious nor national. It is an *existential* community or a set of such communities, born equally at the heart of all wars. In order for this community really to achieve and develop its full existential framework, the refugees and displaced people have to socialize their particular experience of wars, exoduses and camps, however long this takes. Indeed, the timeframe is almost always long – very long.

Different forms of testimony – in postwar tribunals, theatrical representation, declarations made to humanitarian organizations, material from historical research, local or national commemoration – may become a vector in the existential community of refugees finding its voice and socialization.[3] This recognition – a *cultural* one, to be precise – based on narration of the experiences of war, exodus and refuge, would give back to the refugees and displaced the humanity that massacres, destitution, assistance and illegality have successively taken from them.

Far more profound, because closer to life, than the recognition of ethnic or religious differences that monopolize political and media discourse on war – discourses 'from above' and from outside – this recognition would do more than anything else to liberate those concerned from their condition of subordination, inferiority and voiceless exclusion in which millions of refugees and displaced people live throughout the world. Their voice and initiative signal the formation of the subject in the experience of the relief victim: the end of the camp even within the space of the camp itself, the end of de-socialization still within the exodus, an exodus that now takes the form of isolation in the camp or a clandestine existence outside. It would undoubtedly do much in this way to help the conduct of international policy, as the displaced and refugees have buried within them an immense memory of war, revelation of which would contribute to giving a little sense, for everyone, to the violence they have experienced so intimately.

THE MEMORY OF DIRTY WARS

What remains of violence after the worst is escaped? To what point are people still marked physically and morally by the sufferings of war and exodus – internally in their own memories and bodies, and externally in the view of others? If all victims are affected by war and massacre, it is still necessary for this to be known. To be able to give testimony of what has happened helps to give a meaning, a posteriori, to what they have experienced, to socialize it for both themselves and others.

Such testimonies are the premiss for a collective voice, a stammered return to life for those women and men who have lost, temporarily or permanently, their anchorage in the world. They are thus essential to the reconstitution of each individual person. Indissociably with this, however, they have or should have two other consequences in the life of these escapees. One is to create a community of testimony based on shared experiences, trajectories and resemblances: this is the comfort to be expected from immediate exchange, from the tale heard up close. This leads to the beginnings of the existential community that we have just described. The other consequence is more functional: testimony is often needed for the delivery, on the part of various administrative bodies, of rights, titles or documents to refugees, displaced persons, exiles and other sufferers. How can these functions of testimony combine to produce a voice?

Situations of savage violence are the undoubted origin of the difficulty of imagining oneself still alive amid the 'dirty war'. Testimony is a pain, and one not always shared. In May 2000 we met Elena, a thirty-five year old Colombian woman who had arrived in Bogotá a year earlier after fleeing her village in the department of Bolivar, now wholly under the control of the paramilitaries. In the CODHES offices where we conducted this interview were Elena, her sister-in-law from the same village, and a companion who followed them as far as the public body in charge of *desplazados*, where the women had to make their declaration for the third time, after an interval of several months. Despite all that had happened to them, they were still not considered as 'displaced by violence', in the terms used by the Colombian administration.

Elena was a receptionist for the telephone company in her village, in the south of the Bolivar department. Since the mid 1980s the two principal guerrilla groups had controlled the village, but one of these, the Fuerzas Armadas Revolucionarias de Colombia (FARC), had chosen to ally itself with drug traffickers in order to control the production and purchase of coca leaf grown on the village land. Despite occasional clashes between the two rival groups, the villagers lived in relative calm.

In 1997, the arrival of the paramilitaries on the pretext of 'cleaning up' led to a violent conflict for control of local land, villages and narcotraffic. The paramilitaries' targets were those inhabitants suspected of collaboration with the guerrillas, and telephonists were now on the front line; handling communications with the outside world, they were seen as natural accomplices and called '*putas guerrilleras*'. Elena and her colleagues were hunted down, and some of them killed. The massacres affected almost the entire village, and everyone was threatened. Elena fled, first hiding a little way away from the village, then, when the paramilitaries caught up with her, taking flight once more along with her four children and another four nephews and nieces. They went through the forest as the threat also came from the sky; this was the time that army planes were bombing the region in the guise of reprisals against one of the two guerrilla groups, the ELN (Ejercito de Liberación Nacional), which had kidnapped the passengers on an internal air flight that it had hijacked. Elena eventually managed to embark on a rowing boat, and reached Bogotá in this way in May 1999.

Between 1985 and 2000 the city received more than 350,000 displaced people, generally arriving a few at a time and as discreetly as possible, but all making their way to Cuidad Bolivar, and like Elena, to Soacha, outlying quarters whose recent growth is due to the massive arrival of *desplazados*.

It was at this point that the young woman began to give details of the massacres committed by the paramilitaries. 'They cut off one man's head with a power saw; another they cut into several pieces, wrapped him in a hammock and left him outside the house of a relative; they stripped his sister's husband and burned him alive; the *paracos* drink and get high on *bazuco* [a chemical residue left from coca processing] so that they can kill people. . .'

My colleague Edilma Osorio (a sociologist and member of CODHES) and myself stopped asking questions at this point. Elena burst into tears, deep painful sobs, in the midst of tales of massacre and flight that left us speechless. She insisted on telling everything she had seen, but soon she went on to say what she had heard tell, the different episodes following without a break. She spoke, and her sister-in-law echoing, of 'the young women raped and killed', the man 'whose head was cut off and put on a wooden pole', and other atrocities. The interview had become an occasion for catharsis, a redemption in which our three interviewees were united and comforted.

Elena's testimony had the result of convincing a government official, who granted her a card as 'displaced by violence', giving her the right to financial aid for two periods of three months to cover her minimal expenditure on food and lodging, an assistance that displaced persons duly registered by the administration have the right to under a law of 1997 that recognizes their existence and the necessity of humanitarian support.

Tales of this kind, and sometimes just mere lists, seem capable of establishing a common heritage, which could be a 'war memory' if it were more widely socialized. It would be salutary rehabilitation for the displaced if they were recognized as the main depositaries of this collective memory, simply by virtue of their proximity to war. But with the exception of a few circumstances in which people feel they can trust, silence reigns. Even among the dozens of *desplazados*, including our interviewees, who mobilized in the occupation of the Red Cross building in the centre of Bogotá, no one said publicly why they were there. 'Because you don't know who is who, where they come from, you never know who you are speaking to', says Elena. Even here, other people are distrusted, you don't relate the basic events that might constitute a common reference for all those whom the media, the NGOs and researchers call, without really knowing why, the 'community of displaced persons'. Yet there is the material for a common story, one that can strengthen the civilian population in the face of the armed groups that generally monopolize commentary on war.

SEEKING REFUGE

Among the displaced populations, 'disaster victims' as they are called in some countries, it is usual to meet people who seem to have lost their reason, or just the reason for their existence, in the wake of violence and massacre, followed by the losses and traumas of exodus. In the life of the camps, reference to armed conflict remains omnipresent, and explains the frequent persistence of fear and feelings of persecution. Such behaviour has led several medical NGOs to attempt programmes of 'humanitarian psychiatry', especially in refugee camps. Those conducting such programmes are unsure of their effectiveness.

On the one hand, they note that it is never easy to isolate in diagnosis a trauma bound up with war or displacement, to distinguish what doctors among themselves call 'those who are normally ill' from 'those who are abnormally ill'. On the other hand, in the second case, treatment of the suffering caused by war is often linked with an action of testimony: agents of medical organizations have the impression of responding to a need to talk rather than to a demand for psychiatric care in the strict sense. The suffering is reabsorbed in speech, and this merges together with testimony in the trajectory of the victims. Thus Estelle d'Halluin notes with respect to a programme of humanitarian psychiatry in the Gaza strip at the time of the second intifada that 'if medical care is the first justification for the intervention of the psychologist and doctor on the ground, it is joined to concerns of a moral kind . . . The relationship that they establish with the patient is the occasion for a kind of recognition and "re-humanization" of the violated populations.'[4]

This twofold response, medical and moral, to the psychic disturbance caused by war and exodus, can be supplemented by a third, that of re-humanization by the formation of a social context in which individuals can start to 'remake' themselves. This is shown by the examples of Colombia and the Philippines, where displaced people have tried to build 'communities of peace', 'camps of hope', and other zones that establish in their own way pockets of protection within wider regions dominated by war and violence. These are artefacts, therapeutic substitutes for society, creations of social context ex nihilo which, if they endure, will be transformed in due course into genuine spaces of socialization.

But the environment of war makes life hard for these utopias of refuge. The re-settlement of eighty displaced Colombian families in 1997 on the site of La Hacienda La Miel (department of Tolima, in the centre of the country) was requested by the peasants themselves, and obtained from the government department concerned. It followed a collective displacement triggered by massacres and threats from paramilitary groups in the department of Cesar, a few hundred kilometres north of their new installation. This initiative has become exemplary for possible responses to the problem of displaced people, and others have followed.

That same year, two 'communities of peace' saw the light in one of the most violent war zones in Colombia, Urabá in the north-west of the country: one at San José de Apartadó, the other in San Francisco de Asîs. The first of these grouped 1,200 people and the second 4,500, all from nearby villages. In both cases the story was the same: caught in the crossfire of paramilitaries, guerrillas and the government army, the peasants of a number of hamlets sought a 'neutral' municipality in the surrounding region, and applied for protection to representatives of the local government, the Catholic church, and various national and European NGOs. These set up a 'peace community' project that required first of all negotiation with the various armed groups for agreement on a neutral zone where the displaced people could

live. It also envisaged the development of social and economic initiatives for a population strongly marked by the
violence of war and seeking to assert its own neutrality
towards the armed groups: neither to support nor submit to
either camp, and not to use weapons.

These peace communities were in fact entrenched camps,
which have trouble today in gaining recognition from either
the state representatives or the armed groups, despite the
agreements signed. In San José, food aid is supplied by the
municipality and the church; in San Francisco, just by
the church. Physical protection is provided by the peasants
themselves, who do the rounds of their meeting places day
and night, but without weapons, in the name of the principle
of 'peaceful resistance'. The sites where these communities
have been established are, in one case, groups of urban
dwellings whose inhabitants have fled the violence that had
pervaded that sector, and in the other case a camp of *cam-
buches* (shelters of black plastic sheeting).[5]

Two problems immediately appeared: protection and
neutrality. Displaced peasants are suspected of being allies
of the guerrillas, and are closely monitored by the parmili-
taries. On the one hand, they cannot freely enter or leave
their security zone, being confined there by paramilitary
roadblocks that can exact supplies of water, petrol or money,
and prevent the entry of food. On the other hand, the
killing of several of their number by violent groups, whether
paramilitaries or guerrillas, has been facilitated by the suspicion that reigns on all sides, and the absence of a public
security force. If the two peace communities respectively
received one year after their establishment a peace prize
(awarded to the San José community by a US organization)
and a human rights prize (which the French government
gave the San Francisco community), they also suffered the
massacre of their most visible members: in two years, sixty

murders have been committed in San José de Apartadó (eight by the guerrillas, fifty-two by the paramilitaries); and the month of April 1999 alone saw eighteen killings and seven kidnappings among the peace community of San Francisco de Asís.

These attempts seek to make it possible for the civilian populations to continue to live despite their impotence in the face of the conflicts that target them and the meaning of which escape them. Those who have relatives close at hand leave to join them. Those who lack this recourse seek to establish a refuge in impossible no man's lands, semblances of a protected place and social ties that can guarantee their material survival and their psychological equilibrium.

NEW ETHNIC CHEQUERBOARD, NEW EXCHANGES

In the Sudan, certain refugees from neighbouring Eritrea are said to be 'self-settled', that is, living outside the camps. This phenomenon, though large-scale, is hard to assess in quantitative terms. As they receive no humanitarian aid, they have to survive by their own means, and are generally clandestine. Some of them have changed name, language and dress, for the sake of passing unnoticed. In the Islamic northern Sudan, Christians will practise the surrounding religion. Some have made their pilgrimage to Mecca, to be officially recognized as *el Haj*. Gaim Kibreab, who describes this situation, refers here to 'fictional identities'.[6] Devoid of protection, they are in the 'wrong ethnic group', the wrong place, and thus have to pass themselves off as someone else. This does not prevent them from being active in Eritrean politics, and, by circulating more freely in Sudan, being more able than others to circumvent the legal prohibitions of their 'host' country so as to organize political resistance on the part of the dispersed refugees. What we see here is not a loss of identity, but a 'strategy of invisibility'.

Over and above such fictions of identity, it is possible that forced displacement, destitution, and new groupings that are not freely chosen, create extreme contexts propitious for questioning certainties of identity and thus for far-reaching changes. Even if they are not exclusive to this vast world of refugees, such changes are particularly marked in the exodus situation. This is also shown by life in the camps, and in a still more explicit fashion. These social artefacts can become genuine contexts of socialization.

It is tempting, in discussing these changes of identity, to oppose refugees living in town to those installed in the camps. This has been done in a very systematic way by the anthropologist Liisa Malkki, in a research project conducted in the second half of the 1980s among Hutu refugees from Burundi in Tanzania, comparing those living in the Mishamo camp with others 'self-settled' in the town of .Kigoma. The attachment of exiles to their place of departure is respectively stronger or weaker, and the effects of detachment also depend on the places where they settle. Malkki sees settlement as more important than displacement. In this context, she maintains, the camp becomes a reference that is both spatial and 'politico-symbolic': within it, a specific moral and political community is re-established among the Hutu refugees, maintaining its memory and myths of origin. Hutu identity, in fact, is reinforced in the camp. Conversely, those refugees that settle individually in the town display more 'cosmopolitan' forms of identity, and their ethnic identity loses its mythico-historical reference, remaining useful at most in a particular context. The ethno-nationalism of the former is thus countered by the cosmopolitanism of the latter, who may even be seen as agents and originators of a 'post-national order', such as

Arjun Appadurai has maintained. A new world order in which relationships, information and the imaginary would be 'diasporic' in type: refugees, like a network of intellectuals, would experience modernity without a state, 'modernity at large'.[7]

Ethnic and territorial identities at place of origin and in camps, cosmopolitan or fictional identities in urban peripheries; national identities in the first, post-national ones in the second. The experience of the Dadaab camps in Kenya allows us to flesh out and add complexity to an opposition that is too simple as it stands here. To put it in a nutshell, and in a general sense, this example shows how the camp is an experience of identity just as relational and dynamic as that of the non-assisted refugees who have 'self-settled' on the urban periphery.

In the Dadaab camps, some refugees from southern Sudan have established a completely new church, the 'United Church of Christ'. This brings together adherents of the Anglican, Pentecostal, Orthodox and African Inland churches, none of these being numerous enough to conduct their own religious practice. Starting as no more than an accommodation to the constraints of space and number, this pragmatism led to unexpected encounters, and the formation of nothing less than a new religious denomination. This is not exactly a fictional identity, but rather a religious improvisation that relativizes the beliefs of each, an opening of identity that is favourable to transformations.

In the same camps, nationalities become 'ethnicities' in the relational or local sense. Refugees from Ethiopia with various tribal origins, for example, are all identified here as Ethiopian, as too are Eritreans. While stories of war and flight are marked by 'tribal' opposition and violence, and reference to nationality has been deeply abused in ethnic conflicts, the term 'Ethiopian' refers here to a nation simply in terms of place, just like the term 'Sudanese' from which it is differentiated, or again 'Soomaali', a term that groups together here a large number of clan federations, clans and families. These new ethnic terms do not eliminate previous adherence, but they are nonetheless quite genuine terms of identity with a function in the new context. In a certain manner, an arrangement is established that is specific to the camp, a new ethnic chequerboard on which each category is given its meaning and position in relation to the other pieces in place – competing, hostile or allied – and according to the particular rules of the camp.

On this chequerboard, former ethnic balances are transformed and strategies of a new type appear. We can start with a conflict internal to the Soomaalis, who are the numerically dominant group in these camps. Those labelled 'Bantu Soomaalis' are outside of caste, farmers who are pejoratively considered as 'slaves' of the superior groups, among which are the Darood Ogaadeen, numerous in the region and in the camps, who behave arrogantly and dominantly towards them. For centuries those groups considered as inferior saw their identity assimilated to that of the so-called noble clans to which they were affiliated.[8] In the camp, however, the Bantu Soomaalis have been gradually recognized as an autonomous group, detached from the overall Soomaali ethnicity. Their official designation here is simply 'SBR' (Soomaali Bantu Refugees), and they appeal to the camp administration as a 'minority' with the same right as every other (Soomaalis, Sudanese, Ethiopians, etc.) to receive loans for handicraft activities or have access to jobs with the NGOs. The camp thus enables them to shed a devalued intra-ethnic position. Furthermore, this context favours research into ancestral origins that separate them more radically from the Soomaalis and relate them to the countries of Tanzania and Mozambique from where they say they came several centuries back. The representatives of these 'SBRs' have asked the camp administration for collective resettlement in these two countries. This request was refused, but a surprising response came from the United States. Having committed itself to the UN to take its share of refugees, the US administration showed an interest in these Africans attached to their ancestral lands and displaying a great ethnic unity, compatible with the representation of identity that is favoured today in the US. In mid 2000, screening procedures were announced with a view to receiving 10,000 'SBRs' into the United States starting from the end of that year.

This strategy of emancipation from previous powers and invention of an ethnic separatism in the new context of the camp is not unique. It is comparable with the fate of the Twa pygmy group in the refugee camps for Rwandan Hutus at Goma (in the Democratic Republic of Congo, formerly Zaïre) in 1994–6.[9] A minority who were despised by the rest of the population in Rwanda, Hutu and Tutsi alike, the Twa first obtained recognition in the camps. Jean-Pierre Godding says in his introduction to a collection of documents and testimonies by Rwandan refugees that the 5,000 Twa in the camps (out of a total of 750,000 refugees) 'found themselves, just as in Rwanda, the poorest and most marginalized, despised by the others and often excluded from assistance. They managed to develop their own associations and be recognized as such for the distribution of rations; their representatives sat on the committees of some of the camps and obtained a level of recognition that they have never achieved in Rwanda. The UNHCR and certain NGOs made a particular effort in their favour.'[10]

These two examples show how the strategy of strengthening ethnic particularisms is potentially a challenge to existing ethnic domination. This ambivalence of a seemingly traditional strategy can advance to a critique of ethnicity itself. In the Daddab camps, in fact, the dynamic among the Soomaali groups seen as inferior in status and made up of those clans known as 'tradesmen' (*waable*) is not so much ethnic as socio-economic. As members of these castes, craftsmen such as smiths, cobblers, tailors or carpenters fall in with the interest that certain NGOs have in maintaining a semblance of occupation in the life of the camps, so that they support projects of 'income generating activities'. This does not proceed without violence. Craftsmen receiving the support of the NGOs are reminded of their inferior status, and are the object of systematic racketeering by the elders (chiefs) of the higher-status Soomaali clans; others see their workshops destroyed, or are even physically attacked by groups commanded by the 'elders' within the camp.

In this case, the camp does not reinforce ethnicity but, on the contrary, confronts the ethnic question and relativizes it by offering an alternative. The chequerboard with its pieces and specific framework is not strictly ethnic in its rules, but relational in a broader sense. Thus what distinguishes the two superior 'classes' in the social stratification of the camps, the notables and traders on the one hand, the voluntary workers for the NGOs on the other, is the differing weight they give to the ethnic legitimacy of their status: determining and decisive for the Soomaali notables and traders, this is secondary and even criticized among the NGO employees. This competition has the effect of opening up the question of identity, and here again renders the situation somewhat more 'cosmopolitan'.

Other phenomena also contribute to a muddying of ethnic boundaries, e.g. various situations of contact which may be marked by aggressiveness and even occasional physical violence. Yet for all that, these situations present new exchanges, learning experiences, and linguistic and cultural translations, which question the ethnic divisions the refugees have brought with them. With the distribution of shelters, for example, the UNHCR policy is to separate people according to ethnic or clan membership. In the daily life of the refugees, however, encounters take place in the market, round the wells, at the food distribution centre or the health posts, some of which would have been unthinkable before the camp on account of ethnic separation or conflict. The Soomaali elders tried without success to close down the video shops and coffee shops run by Ethiopians, and many young Soomaalis can now be found there. Some Ethiopian refugees, the great majority of whom are young men, arrive single and find wives among women from Somalia, who are then rejected by their own community. Groups of Soomaalis even enter the Ethiopian quarter to take women of their own ethnicity by force, leaving the husband with the couple's children, whom they view as illegitimate in their patrilineal notion of kinship. But these marriages continue. . .

As soon as they are settled for a while, and each person is forced to seek their bearings, however provisional, the camps transform themselves, and transform the lives of those living in them. They represent a new context, and to a certain point an innovatory one, even if such changes involve suffering and are the occasion of personal conflict.

In Africa, a continent where the ethnic or cultural origin of wars is more often asserted than actually proved (as we have seen above), we can maintain that, among the refugees themselves, confronted with the evidence of the heterogeneity of their societies of origin, ethnic relations are redefined and life in the camps creates new identities, both ethnic and non-ethnic. Given the material precariousness and social instability, this represents a particular apprenticeship in reflexivity, a distancing from one's own identity and an experience of change. In this sense, the camps embody a modernity pushed to excess: synonymous with an overthrow of certainties of identity that are local and immemorial, and confrontation with difference, competition and exchange. This existence in turn provides new bearings of identity, new cultural apprenticeships.

CONFRONTATION, DISTURBANCE AND DEBATE

Rapes take place in the camps, but also outside – around ten per month reported in the first half of 2000 according to the registers of the camp police, though this number is by general opinion below the real figure. The victims are women who travel a few kilometres out in search of wood for cooking. Some NGOs (Care, the Ted Turner Foundation, the National Council of Churches of Kenya) run information and prevention programmes on 'gender relations', 'reproductive health' and 'sexual violence'. But this is a recurrent theme in discussions between the UNHCR security services, the Kenyan police and the refugee representatives, principally Soomaalis.

A security meeting was held on 28 June 2000 in one of the three UNHCR camps at Dadaab, in the presence of eighty refugees (thirty-five women, forty-five men), who met with ten other individuals (two Kenyan police officers, three officials from the UNHCR security service, four social workers from Care and myself). On the agenda: 'mobilize young people to escort women going to collect firewood'.

NGO officials and police accused Soomaali men of not arranging for women of their ethnic group to be defended, while refusing to go out and look for wood themselves; some Soomaali refugees are even suspected, more discreetly, of being themselves involved in rape, actively or complicitly. Southern Sudanese men go out to collect wood instead of women, a fact that they emphasized in the course of the

meeting. The refugees of all ethnic groups accused the
Kenyan police of not escorting the women, and the police
replied that in case of rape they would then be accused themselves! Above all, the refugees complain of not being given
weapons to protect their women in the bush: 'Unarmed
escorts are no use at all', one Soomaali woman insists, 'the
bush rapists are armed, and they also enter the camp blocks
armed. If you cry out, they kill you, and though the police are
in the camps, they don't come into the blocks.' In these conditions, a Soomaali representative notes, 'to ask young people
to escort women would lead to massacres as well as rapes. . .
as refugees, we are unable to leave the camp'.

In a general manner, all the refugees who spoke at the
meeting demanded more in the way of security measures.
Some of these were agreed (more police, strengthening of
fences), others refused (weapons for refugees undertaking the
escort of women, possibilities of establishing radio communi-
cation to raise the alarm in case of an incident in a block).

This meeting did not lead to any definite response to the
problem of rape, any more than has been the case on other
occasions. But this did become a theme of discussion, and
despite the reticence of some Soomali elders, there was the
beginning of a public debate. A change that affects inhabitants of all ethnic groups can thus come about by questioning on the basis of everyday evidence the contexts of
interpretation and action with which each person has arrived
on these UNHCR sites, international and multi-ethnic as
they are.

Exodus, migration, and in this case also the camp itself,
generate experiences of socialization that put many levels of
determination in contact, in accelerated fashion and in one
and the same space: clan strategies come up against ethnic
strategies, which themselves confront those of 'global' aid
organizations that are more or less influential according to

whether individuals are inside the camp or not, and in more or less constraining situations. Besides, different choices are available to the NGOs, for example opposing those who favour integration, dialogue and sometimes direct encounter between people whose origins lie in enemy groups, to those who seek to avoid contacts that may lead to conflict, and therefore separate and isolate different groups, winkle out 'false refugees' among the local populations that approach the camps, and promote departure – in a word, those who conceive the camps solely as an emergency police measure. The consequence of this experience is a rapid change in the composition of the cultural, political, and identity frameworks of the refugees.

On the morning of 1 July 2000, in the three UNHCR camps at Dadaab, the employees of the UN World Food Programme began the distribution of rations of maize, lentils, oil and salt for the 124,000 refugees, as they had done every two weeks, under the watchful eye of some Soomaali elders, cane or umbrella in hand, and the active participation of leaders of the camp's sections or quarters, who are younger and belong to several ethnic groups. Organized by the Canadian NGO Care, they are recognizable by their blue shirts. But on this occasion the routine was interrupted when the refugees from Somalia started to parade up and down with songs and cries of joy. In one of the camps, on the wide dusty ground that separates the buildings of the aid organizations from the dwellings of the refugees, hundreds of children, young people and adults were running and making merry behind the blue-starred Somalian flag.

They were commemorating in this way the independence of their country of origin on 1 July 1960. Some people also said, and the rumour quickly spread, that an agreement had just been signed, in the context of the negotiations under way in Djibouti, for a return to peace and an understanding

between the different clans with a view to forming a government of reconciliation in Mogadishu. A Soomaali elder,
interrupting his control of the distribution of provisions,
improvised a short speech in which he thanked the United
Nations, the UNHCR, and the aid organizations for the
assistance they had provided the refugees in Dadaab for
nearly a decade, and announced that they would now be able
to return home soon. He was only waiting to see the writ-
ten confirmation of the news after hearing it on the BBC
World Service, which broadcasts two news programmes a
day in Soomaali.

Later on in the day, the demonstrators met up in the
centre of the same patch of ground. Near an almost bare
tree – on which a dozen or so children were perched, like
any other place in the village – three young leaders, a woman
and two elders were addressing a large and excited public
through loudspeakers they had somehow obtained. One
spoke of peace, and the unity of the Somalian people.
Another took the microphone to declaim improvised poems
in homage to peace and his country. A third wanted his message to be heard by the Djibouti conference, and asked for it
to be recorded on cassette for transmission to the BBC: here,
he said, several Soomaali clans had come together and lived
as good neighbours; the whole country could do likewise. In
the camp, the Somali Youth League, founded in 1943 and
the main agent of Somalian independence in 1960, has
become the Somali Youth League for Reconciliation. It is
run by young refugees working for the Canadian organization Care.

The agreement on the formation of a government of
unity to restore peace between the clans was not in fact
reached that day, nor the day after. But if negotiations continue on the path of national political reconciliation, Somalians who today are refugees in the adjoining countries of

Kenya and Ethiopia will gradually be invited to return to their country. As against all the official declarations, however, it is likely that a large number of the refugees at Dadaab no longer want to return 'home' to Somalia. Some of them because it is so long ago that they left, as far back as the late 1970s, and they feel too old now to resettle in places where they have nothing. Others because they have distanced themselves somewhat from the ethnic memberships that structure their country of origin; formed in the proximity of the international NGOs, they find it hard to envisage their departure from the camps in which they have been socialized for more than ten years.

More generally, the discovery of institutions and values that come from afar and arrived along with the humanitarian aid has made the camps into contexts of life that, despite being sedentary and geographically isolated, rapidly become globalized and induce definite cultural changes. In the Rwandan refugee camps at Goma (Democratic Republic of the Congo), although the UNHCR camp administration, under pressure from the former Zaïrean government, had banned most commercial, social and cultural activity, thirty-five associations were subsequently formed in less than two years. With the particular support of Catholic NGOs, various committees, circles, communities, teams and other discussion groups enabled the Rwandan refugees, who were chiefly Hutu, to debate, exchange or write their reflections on the themes of peace, non-violence, forgiveness and reconciliation.

In the Dadaab camps, there have been protests against the humanitarian organizations, leading to a basic political relationship between the refugees and the NGOs on the subject of aid. Thus May–June 2000 saw a protest against the poor quality of food ration products, which was marked by one group of refugees refusing to accept their rations, and explaining this to the BBC World Service, so that this 'boycott' of humanitarian aid became known throughout East Africa. A few months earlier, refugees who were 'volunteer workers' for particular NGOs went on strike for about ten days in order to win a remuneration equal to that paid by other international organizations: they obtained rises that averaged 20 per cent.

When they arrive in the camps, the refugees begin to experience new situations: diversities of languages, values and information, direct discussion with the agents of international organizations. To differing degrees the meetings, protests and debate described here illustrate a process of *local globalization*. This is not necessarily bound up with any great mobility for individuals, rather with a change of 'scale', a rapprochement between the global and the local that they experience in their everyday lives. This globalization in the camps also takes a further important form: the appearance of comparative judgements on an international level rather than a purely local one. The announcement in 1999 of 'what a refugee costs', again something heard on the BBC World Service, aroused comments that remained in the memory of the people at Dadaab. This cost was estimated at the time at one US dollar a day, but in a stably established camp such as Dadaab it is much less, maybe as low as 50 cents. The publicity that this announcement and the ensuing commentaries received assumed that it was perfectly legitimate to compare the life of a Somalian refugee in this camp, not with the cost of policies of village development in the surrounding region, but with the 'cost' of a Kosovan refugee in Europe, which is around US $10 a day.

RESCUES

The great majority of those who eventually find themselves with no other identity save that of displaced persons or refugees are 'local' rather than 'global', if we use the terms proposed by sociologist Zygmunt Bauman to denote a social categorization on the world scale.[11] Their material and symbolic existence depends on a stable local anchorage; they are unfamiliar with the rapid, multilingual and border-less world of the 'globals' – the agents of globalization who form a socially homogeneous elite. The 'locals', for their part, lack all of the skills needed for that world.

The irremediable locality of their socialization, followed by violent removal from the sites of that identity, renders the majority of refugees quite fragile in the context of their forced exodus. But some transferable skills enable certain of their number to escape the fate of the majority, sometimes at the cost of cynical experiences. Thus the outcome most sought after by the refugees in East Africa, that of resettlement in a 'First World' country, generally gives rise, in the refugee camps themselves, to a minute and unofficial examination known as 'screening': state of health, educational level, professional training, language skills, age and sex are noted for each individual who requests reception 'in a third country', as well as the sole criterion officially recorded by the UNHCR, that of the refugee's safety.

At a certain point Canada was well disposed to the resettlement of women refugees from Sudan, in order to balance the demographic composition of its population. Australia very clearly signposts the criterion of 'suitability for social integration' in its own screening, and the refugees are well aware that this means the educational level of candidates. The United States selected the refugees it accepted from an ethnic group that appeared more cohesive and united than others, and attached to its land of origin.[12] On the other hand, a young Somalian, Mohammad, a second-year student of medicine when he fled the war in Mogadishu, tells how he passed an 'oral test' for possible resettlement in the

United States, and everything was going well, until he 'tripped up' on a single question. When he was asked if he wanted to return eventually to Africa, he answered with a sincere and enthusiastic 'no', understanding only too late that his examiners would rather have heard 'yes' as a proof of attachment to his original identity. This mistake, as Mohammad sees it, is responsible for the fact that he was not accepted and is still living in a Kenyan refugee camp.

There are certainly ethnic factors that make it possible for certain groups to live clandestinely outside the camps, away from their land of origin, and reorganize themselves sooner than others. This is the case with the Soomaalis concentrated in the 'Soomaali' quarter of Nairobi where they work in the informal economy, or that of the Gypsy networks of Bosnia. Within these partly nomadic populations, individual dramas of war, loss, even the destruction of their places of origin, are partly resolved as a function of the delocalized and transnational networks of their ethnic group.[13] This is then a case of human rescue and temporary arrangements that ensure a minimal social life, illegal though it may be: false nationality papers, child labour, illegal occupation of housing or land, clandestine workshops, prostitution. Moral condemnation does not help matters, nor subsequent punishment. Here again it is only the survivors whom we meet. The others remain perfect victims who can be pitied without risk. What can we say then of those who remain alive no matter what the cost? Who claim a right to life outside legal norms and contexts that they are precisely refused?

There is a right to life in illegality. Local wars, abandonment and destitution face millions of individuals each day with the question of mere survival. They resolve this by an improvised hotchpotch of solutions to their physical, biological and social destitution, solutions that are generally clandestine, but this minimal life legitimates a social illegality.

This can only embarrass the 'proper' rich world: let them die or let them act? This embarrassment will persist as long as the countries of the 'First World' do not feel concerned by this human (or should we say 'inhuman') dimension of the present international order.

VICTIM AND SUBJECT

To survive, therefore, the choice is between playing the victim or acting illegally. Humanitarian aid and illegality are the two permanent markers in personal strategies of survival and political action by these exiles from dirty wars. One is marked by the intervention, sometimes on a massive scale, of UN organizations and international NGOs. The other takes shape in the gaps left by humanitarian intervention, or in its absence. It is here, in heterodox political action and beyond immediate demands (for physical survival and a framework of resocialization), that the cultural recognition of their experience of war, violence and exodus is most overtly and publicly played out.

On 14 December 1999, several hundred *desplazados* invaded the offices of the International Committee of the Red Cross, in the centre of Bogotá – an occupation which, as we saw above, lasted over a year and made a great deal of disturbance.

The political action of the Colombian *desplazados* started after the passing of a new law in 1997 that recognized the status of displaced people as a basis for certain possible rights. The occupation of the Red Cross offices had in fact been preceded by several 'seizures' of major points in the city: a church, the interior ministry, the presidential department responsible for the question of displaced people, the offices of the UNHCR. These were certainly tactics of desperation, since their origin was the need to obtain immediate assistance, food, and shelter – complaints that could lead to a violent or media-directed occupation without a specific plan having been made in advance. An illegal occupation of this kind becomes an apprenticeship in politics.

Two weeks after the arrival of the first occupiers, over a thousand *desplazados* had established themselves in the ICRC building and the street outside. This street, rapidly closed to traffic by the forces of order, was claimed by the occupiers, who set up plastic tents, did their cooking on wood fires, washed their clothes and began to live there as they might have done in a formalized camp. After a few days, the '*invasión*' was encircled by the police, who controlled all the exits, and the comings and goings of the occupiers. Between two and three hundred thus remained 'prisoners of their own occupation', as they themselves put it, until the beginning of 2001.

After a month of occupation and a first round of negotiation with representatives of the public services responsible for the question of displaced people, a preliminary agreement was signed providing for emergency financial support to cover the housing and food expenses of the *desplazados*: three months' rent, a three-month food basket, and enrolment of children in the state schools. But the occupiers wanted more: support for definitive resettlement in the city, and the financing of 'productive projects'. In the midst of this movement, an inquiry among 250 occupiers of the Red Cross building, three-quarters of whom were of rural origin, showed that the majority wanted to resettle in the city, 75 per cent precisely in Bogotá, rather than returning home.

After the ICRC had moved its base of operations to another building in the city, the last *desplazados*, somewhere over 150, obtained some new successes, though these were small given the duration of the conflict, and were only thanks to a legal action: food aid was now to be extendable in principle for a second period of three months, and additional housing aid was granted. After the conflict proper came to an end in March 2001, fifty families remained in the building, which they transformed into a squat.

In the course of the movement the legitimacy of the *desplazados* was rapidly challenged on all sides: its spokespeople were discredited, some for supposed links with the guerrilla movement (two of them did in fact tell us that they were very close to it), others because they were seen as marginal drug-addicts, former workers in the coca fields or street-dwellers in Bogotá (which one of them was), or again suspected of being 'phoney' displaced people and in fact peasant activists; all were said to lack experience and called irresponsible agitators. In general, faced with this occupation at the very heart of the capital, and of an NGO that is among those with the best reputation in the world for its assistance to displaced people, refugees and the helpless, the media and the general population swung between compassion aroused by the spectacle of such utter destitution, and rejection of a population that always threatened to sully them.

The major aid organizations and churches have always been involved with the movement of displaced people, in Colombia as elsewhere. For the *desplazados*, the NGOs under siege may be mere mediators, a sounding board, or a protective shield from behind which they address themselves in fact to the government. But it is not clear that this was the only motive. The establishment of the UNHCR in Colombia in 1999, for example, provided a direct and immediate target, as an organ of social provision in the context of internal war. In the same sense, in the refugee camps the UNHCR loses the aura of benevolence it has in the 'First World' and is perceived by the 'assisted' as a police force and authority in charge of their sites. The refugees and displaced people do indeed therefore face a *globalization* of their political interlocutors, at the same time as a sharp confrontation with nation-states, from the painful experience they have of national borders, and from their quest for institutional recognition and the rights associated with this. In this sense, the exodus has precipitated them into modernity and into a form of political action that is both national and more globalized than their previous life ever was.

In its very 'impurity', this population born of war and violence represents civil society as it actually is, in the only form in which this can exist in time of war, one that conforms very little to the dream of a civil society that is innocent, enlightened, and not linked with conflict. Habituation to violence, the impunity of political violence, the real links between political and social violence, have all made the situation of countries at war more complex, with a considerable deterioration in their social organization. In Colombia, the involvement of the *desplazados* in political action is an elementary reminder of their right to life, a right that the illegal armed groups do not recognize, whilst the public authorities are reluctant to give them social recognition, still less cultural. The action just described has shown political actors who are unaccustomed to this role, unpredictable in negotiations, confused in the organization of their movement, and heterogeneous in both their social characteristics and their political slant, but above all they are suspected of bearing within them the very causes that have brought them to this point. Yet it is on the basis of this political action for vital objectives that the *desplazados* began to be recognized, and differentiated from the armed groups who are seen as the only political subjects of the 'conflict'. The formation of a national coordination of *desplazados* in March 2000, in which the occupiers of the Red Cross building participated, is interesting from this point of view.

It is by appearing as political subjects, however unexpected their forms of expression and their demands, that the 'communities' of displaced people and refugees become identifiable in society.

The highly symbolic and dramatic forms of expression of the Bogotá *desplazados* – crucifying themselves, lying down in the middle of the street, weeping before the cameras, placing their children up front, hunger strikes – attest to the double reality that is common to victims of all wars: the silence to which violence has condemned its victims, and the attempt at emancipation and expression of the subject in a broad political space, the space of the world.

In Bogotá as at Goma, Gaza or Dadaab, speech represents an arrival in the field of politics, at the same time as it enables recognition of existential communities and contributes to the rescue of each individual life. Those who have escaped and survived the threats facing them find a meaning in their experience from the moment that their story is recognized as a voice – audible in the public space of the town, street corners, television, the papers, tribunals – and not only as suffering.

5

CONCLUSION: WHAT REFUGEES NEED IS FAME

Only fame will eventually answer the repeated complaint of refugees of all social strata that 'nobody knows who I am'; and it is true that the chances of the famous refugees are improved, just as a dog with a name has a better chance to survive than a stray dog who is just a dog in general.

Hannah Arendt[1]

Refugees and 'big men' live in the same world as we ourselves. This 'we' includes both writers and their readers, it includes those who decide on humanitarian action, and those who are its spectators or contributors. If it places 'us' in an external situation to the refugees of whom 'we' speak, this externality is simply one more aspect of the overall distancing that the refugees, and all those receiving humanitarian assistance, face. The steamroller of the great security segregation places 'us' in immunized spaces that are ever more watertight thanks to our social and police protection. Our intercourse, free and democratic as it may be, is amputated by being closed off in this way (whether by our own decision or not) by both visible and invisible protective walls, which keep us at a distance from those of whom we speak. There is a strong chance, in the present logic of the imperial system (and insofar as this logic is passively accepted) that 'we' shall be increasingly less likely to have any direct social connection or intellectual exchange with those who are 'shut out', as either 'vulnerable' or 'undesirable' or both, so that we could check the accuracy and effectiveness of our analyses.

Two conclusions follow from this. First of all, the intellectual deconstruction of these notions and the practices that they sustain, whether cynically or in good faith, is necessary in order to establish a community of speech 'without borders': the vulnerable, the wretched, and all other kinds of absolute victim, are not subjects of speech. The model imposed on them is that of silent victim, in the sense in which human rights as these apply to victim identities give no political rights, and it will only disappear when the 'international community' – a new type of institutional subject – so decides. Secondly, if we can understand that 'we' are also affected by the global security segregation – though in our case, of course, with very different effects, seemingly quite opposite ones for our condition of existence from those of the refugee populations –, this will mean that the scale of that 'organic solidarity' which Durkheim saw as the motive force of social functioning has been globalized. In this sense we are certainly in 'solidarity' with the refugees, a de facto solidarity no matter where they are to be found. There is an intellectual urgency to discover the cultural and political consequences of this solidarity of fate.

I return to the words of Hannah Arendt: what the refugees need is fame. Only a political space and political speech can return those who are nameless and voiceless in our common world.

Already from afar we can see the 'shore on which unknown men and women wait indefinitely to leave for a country that does not exist'.[2] We speak of it with charity, to be sure, and potentially with compassion, but without seeing that today's extreme modernity, with its segregations, hatreds, and wars without end, has placed this shore at the heart of reflection on the future of our common planet. We have to rediscover the unity of the human condition in the face of the withdrawal of some and the quarantine of others – an anthropological urgency that we all have to share.

Chapter 1 Introduction

1 The UNHCR reported 130,000 'invisible' refugees in Pakistan as of 3 November 2001, i.e. less than a month after the start of the US military campaign in Afghanistan and while the frontier was closed, preventing the flow of refugees into the very camps prepared for their reception (*Le Monde*, 4 November 2001).

2 Research conducted in the context of the Institut de Recherche pour le Développement, Paris. Investigation on the ground was made possible by the friendly help of Fernando Urrea of the Universidad de Valle (UNI-VALLE, Cali) and Flor Edilma Osorio (Universidad Javeriana, Bogotá) in Colombia, and of Médecins Sans Frontières (French and Belgian sections) in the refugee camps of sub-Saharan Africa.

Chapter 2 Bruised Populations

1 These figures are of course approximate and in some cases open to question; they leave out, for instance, a large but

necessarily unknown number of refugees who have not declared themselves as such and have immigrated illegally into foreign countries. See in particular the UNHCR publication *Fifty Years of Humanitarian Action* (2000) and its annual survey *The State of the World's Refugees*.

2 B. Bogdanovic, 'L'urbicide ritualisé', quoted and commented by O. Mongin, *Vers la troisième ville?*, Paris: Hachette 1995, p. 63. See also F. Chaslin, *Une haine monumentale, Essai sur la destruction des villes en ex-Yougoslavie*, Paris: Descartes and Cie 1997.

3 A. Politovskaya, *A Small Corner of Hell: Despatches from Chechnya*, Chicago: Chicago University Press 2003.

4 On the genocide of the Rwandan Tutsis in 1994, and the conduct of 'pure inhumanity' that this involved, see C. Vidal, 'Le genocide des Rwandais tutsis: cruauté délibérée et logiques de haine', in F. Héritier (ed.), *De la violence*, Paris: Odile Jacob, 1996, pp. 223–71, and 'Les configurations de l'espace, du temps et de la subjectivité dans un contexte de terreur: l'exemple colombien', *Cultures et Conflits*, no. 37, 2000, pp. 123–54.

5 See CODHES, *Un país que huye. Desplazamiento y violencia en una nación fragmentada*, Bogotá, CODHES/UNICEF, 1999.

6 According to CODHES (Consultoria para los Derechos Humanos y el Desplazamiento), a Colombian NGO established in 1992 to monitor the development of forced displacement and the only body that has so far managed to give quantitative assessments of this phenomenon, the cumulative total of forced displacements between 1985 and 2000 is more than 2,100,000 people. These figures have been challenged, but no other reliable data have been offered. It is clear that such assessment is difficult, not simply for 'technical' reasons of recording displacement, but also for political reasons bound up with the bad

international image of a country that generates such ominous figures, and more prosaically, the length of time for which the *desplazados* are assisted. Under the law of 1997 that recognizes their right to humanitarian aid, a *desplazado* is recognized as such and offered assistance for three months, with the possibility of a further three-month period. After this time they are no longer seen as 'displaced'.

7 See CODHES, *Un país que huye*, op. cit.

8 See K. Peters and P. Richards, 'Jeunes combattants parlant de la guerre et de la paix en Sierra Leone', *Cahiers d'Études Africaines*, nos. 150–2, 1998, pp. 581–617.

9 1991, a year of war in Somalia, was also a year of great famine.

10 This category has not been identified as such by international bodies, even if the question of responsibility for these 'IDPs' (Internally Displaced Persons) is not yet settled.

11 *The Promise* and *Rosetta*, films by Luc and Jean-Pierre Dardenne (Belgium 1996, 1999). *La Vendedora de Rosas*, film by Victor Gaviria (Colombia 1998).

12 In his article 'Un people de deux millions d'êtres est devenu libre', *Le Monde*, 25 March 2000.

13 C. Bernand, 'Ségrégation et anthropologie, anthropologie de la ségrégation. Quelques elements de réflexion', in J. Brun and C. Rhein (eds), *La Ségrégation dans la ville. Concepts et measures*, Paris: L'Harmattan, 1994, p. 78.

14 M. Douglas, *De la Souillure. Essai sur les notions de pollution et de tabou*, Paris: Maspero, 1971.

15 C. Bernand, op. cit., p. 78.

16 *Diners*, 16 May 2000.

17 See R. Bazenguissa-Ganga, 'Les milices politiques dans les affrontements', *Afrique Contemporaine*, no. 186, 1998, pp. 46–57.

18 See C. Lévi-Strauss, *L'Identité*, Paris: PUF, 1977, p. 332.

19 H. Arendt, *The Human Condition*, Chicago: Chicago University Press 1970, p. 26.

20 Ibid.

Chapter 3 The Desert, the Camp, the City

1 H. Arendt, *Qu'est-ce que la politique?* (ed. U. Ludz), Paris: Seuil 1995, p. 144.

2 *Réfugiés Rwandais au Zaïre, Sommes-nous encore des hommes?* A collection of documents from the discussion groups in the camps, introduced and presented by J.-P. Godding, Paris: L'Harmattan, 1997, p. 45.

3 L. Cambrezy, *Réfugiés et exilés. Crise des sociétés, crise des territoires*, Paris: Éditions des Archives Contemporaines, 2001, p. 72. These percentages are based on a figure of four million refugees assisted by the UNHCR. No complete and reliable data are available for the total number of refugees sheltered in the camps.

4 R. Brauman, *Humanitaire: le dilemme*, interview with P. Petit, Paris: Textuel, 1996, p. 43.

5 In J.-C. Rufin's terms; see 'Les économies de guerre dans les conflits internes', in F. Jean and J.-C. Rufin (ed.), *Économie des guerres civiles*, Paris: Hachette, pp. 19–59.

6 See M. Le Pape, 'La presse et les réfugiés rwandais au Congo-Zaïre (octobre 1996-août 1997)', *Afrique Contemporaine*, no. 183, 1997, pp. 57–66.

7 These 'Bantu Soomaalis' are outside the caste system, in other words minorities of non-Soomaali origin, immigrant farmers traditionally considered as serfs or slaves of the higher Soomaali groups.

8 See M. de Certeau, *L'Invention du quotidien*, Paris: Gallimard, 1980.

9 See N. Gomes, 'Solidarité et réseaux dans l'exil. Les réfugiés somaliens clandestins au Kenya et en Éthiopie',

in L. Cambrezy and V. Lassailly-Jacob (eds), *Populations réfugiées. De l'exil au retour*, Paris: Éditions de l'IRD, 2001, pp. 301–19.

10 According to a study by the Save the Children Fund on the health and food economy at Dadaab in 1999 (P. Couts et al., *Kenya Refugee Study Food Economy. Updates of Ifo, Dagahaley and Hagadera Refugee Camps, Dadaab*, Final Report, Save the Children Fund, Nairobi, September 1999, 21-page manuscript).

11 Since the 1980s the term NIMBY ('not in my own back yard') has been used to denote the movement of private municipalization invented by white middle-class residents of Los Angeles. (See M. Davis, *City of Quartz*, London: Verso 1990.)

12 M. Augé, *Non-lieux. Introduction à une anthropologie de la surmodernité*, Paris: Seuil, 1992.

13 B. Geremek, *Les Marginaux parisiens aux XIVe et XVe siècles*, Paris: Flammarion, 1976, p. 204.

14 Ibid., p. 207.

15 G. Agamben, *Homo Sacer: Sovereign Power and Bare Life*, Stanford: Stanford University Press 1998, p. 182 (translation modified).

16 Ibid.

17 See J. Rancière, 'Biopolitique ou politique?', *Multitudes*, no. 1, March 2000, pp. 88–93.

18 Ibid., p. 90.

19 H. Arendt, *The Human Condition*, op. cit., p. 26.

20 M. Agier, *L'Invention de la ville. Banlieues, townships, invasions et favelas*, Paris: Éditions des Archives contemporaines, 1999, p. 31.

21 On the retention of foreigners at the gates of Europe, the Migreurop network maintains and distributes a map of such holding camps, available on the site *http:/www/migreurop.org*.

Chapter 4 The Right to Life

1 Starting from testimonies from the survivors of Nazi camps, Michael Pollak has demonstrated the 'common awareness of an existential difference' among those he interviewed. (In *L'Éxperience concentrationnaire. Essai sur le maintien de l'identité sociale*, Paris: Métailié 2000 [1990], p. 13.)

2 Cf. C. Lévi-Strauss (ed.), *L'Identité*, op. cit., p. 10.

3 To judge, heal the past, and at the same time rebuild a broken society, is the aim of commissions proposed in many countries that have experienced internal war, after the South African model. One of the first decisions of Nelson Mandela after the end of apartheid was to set up the Truth and Reconciliation Commission.

4 E. d'Halluin, *Guerre et psychiatrie. L'intervention humanitaire en Palestine*, Mémoire de DEA, Paris: EHEES, 2001. See also B. Dora, *L'Inhumanitaire, ou le cannibalisme guerrier à l'ère néolibérale*, Paris: La Dispute, 2000. The present notes are also inspired by Yuven Alis, a psychiatric nurse for Médecins Sans Frontières who escorted me in the Dadaab camps, and the discussions we had on this subject.

5 See the dossier published by Oxfam UK, a contributor to these programmes, in E. Hernández Delgado and M. Salazar Posada, *Con la esperanza intacta. Experiencias comunitarias de resistencia civil no violenta*, Bogotá: Oxfam 1999.

6 G. Kibreab, 'Revisiting the Debate on People, Place, Identity and Displacement', *Journal of Refugee Studies*, vol. 12/4, 1999, pp. 384–428.

7 See L. Malkki, *Purity and Exile: Violence, Memory and National Cosmology Among Hutu Refugees in Tanzania*, Chicago: Chicago University Press 1995; idem, 'Refugees and Exile: From "refugee studies" to the national order of

things', *Annual Review of Anthropology*, no. 24, 1995, pp. 495–523; A. Appadurai, *Modernity at Large. Cultural Dimensions of Globalization*, Minneapolis: University of Minnesota Press, 1996.

8 See M. Mohamed-Abdi, 'Les bouleversements induits de la guerre civile en Somalie: castes marginales et minorities', *Autrepart*, no. 15, 2000, pp. 131–47.

9 Following the genocide of Rwandan Tutsis (April–July 1994) and the seizure of power in Kigali by the Hutu-backed Rwanda Patriotic Front in July 1994, nearly one and a half million Rwandans, mainly Hutus, fled to the Congo in fear of reprisals. Some 750,000 of these were held in the Goma camps until November 1996, when they were returned to Rwanda by the Rwandan authorities allied with the rebel armed forces of Laurent-Desiré Kabila, before he took power in Kinshasa.

10 *Réfugiés rwandais au Zaïre*, op. cit., p. 36.

11 Z. Bauman, *Globalization: The Human Consequences*, Cambridge: Polity 1998.

12 This was the new minority of Soomaali Bantu Refugees (see above).

13 See N. Gomes, op. cit., and F. Bouillon, 'L'après-guerre de Bosnie. Conditions de vie et processus de fragilisation de familles bosno-tsiganes dans une cité marseillaise', *Études Tsiganes*, 14, 2000, pp. 57–70.

5 Conclusion

1 Hannah Arendt, *The Origins of Totalitarianism*, New York: Harcourt Brace Jovanovich 1968, p. 287.

2 J. M. G. Le Clézio, *La Quarantaine*, Paris: Gallimard 1995, p. 159.

BIBLIOGRAPHY

Books

Agamben, Giorgio, *Homo Sacer: Sovereign Power and Bare Life*, Stanford: Stanford University Press, 1998.

Agier, Michel, *L'Invention de la ville. Banlieues, townships, invasions et favelas*, Paris: Éditions des Archives contemporaines, 1999.

Appadurai, Arjun, *Modernity at Large. Cultural Dimension of Globalization*, Minneapolis, University of Minnesota Press, 1996.

Arendt, Hannah, *The Origins of Totalitarianism*, New York: Harcourt Brace Jovanovich, 1968.

——*The Human Condition*, Chicago: Chicago University Press, 1970.

——*Qu'est-ce que la politique?* (ed. U. Ludz), Paris: Seuil, 1995.

Augé, Marc, *Non-lieux. Introduction à une anthropologie de la surmodernité*, Paris: Seuil, 1992.

Bauman, Zygmunt, *Globalization: The Human Consequences*, Cambridge: Polity, 1998.

Boltanski, Luc, *La Souffrance à distance. Morale humanitaire, medias et politique*, Paris: Métailié, 1993.

Brauman, Rony, *Humanitaire: le dilemme*, interview with Philippe Petit, Paris: Textuel, 1996.

Cambrezy, Luc, *Réfugiés et exilés. Crise des sociétés, crise des territoires*, Paris: Éditions des Archives contemporaines, 2001.

Certeau, Michel de, *L'Invention du quotidien. 1. Manières de faire*, Paris: Gallimard, 1980.

Chaslin, François, *Une haine monumentale. Essai sur la destruction des villes en ex-Yougoslavie*, Paris: Descartes and Cie, 1997.

Cigerli, Sabri, *Les Réfugiés kurdes d'Irak en Turquie*, Paris: L'Harmattan, 1998.

Davis, Mike, *City of Quartz*, London: Verso, 1990.

Doray, Bernard, *L'Inhumanitaire, ou le cannibalisme guerrier à l'ère néolibérale*, Paris: La Dispute, 2000.

Geremek, Bronislaw, *Les Marginaux parisiens aux XIVe et XVe siècles*, Paris: Flammarion, 1976.

Godding, Jean-Pierre (ed.), *Réfugiés rwandais au Zaïre*, Paris: L'Harmattan, 1997.

Jean, François and Rufin, Jean-Christopher (eds), *Économie des guerres civiles*, Paris: Hachette, 1996.

Lassailly-Jacob, Véronique (ed.), *Communautés déracinées dans les pays du Sud*, *Autrepart* no. 5, Éditions de l'Aube, 1998.

Lassailly-Jacob, Véronique, Marchal, Jean-Yves, and Quesnel, André (eds), *Déplacés et réfugiés. La mobilité sous contrainte*, Paris: Éditions de l'IRD, 1999.

Le Clézio, J. M. G., *La Quarantaine*, Paris: Gallimard, 1995.

Malkki, Liisa, *Purity and Exile: Violence, Memory and National Cosmology Among Hutu Refugees in Tanzania*, Chicago: Chicago University Press, 1995.

Mongin, Olivier, *Vers la troisième ville?*, Paris: Hachette, 1995.

Politkovskaya, Anna, *A Small Corner of Hell: Despatches from Chechnya*, Chicago: Chicago University Press, 2003.

Pollak, Michael, *L'Expérience concentrationnaire. Essai sur le maintien de l'identité sociale*, Paris: Métailié, 2000 [1990].

Rancière, Jacques, *Aux bords du politique*, Paris: La Fabrique-Éditions, 1998.

Rapoport, Michel, *Les Réfugiés. Parias ou citoyens*, Paris: Le Monde/Marabout, 1998.

Sluka, Jeffrey A. (ed.), *Death Squad. The Anthropology of State Terror*, Philadelphia: University of Pennsylvania Press, 2000.

Articles and Reports

Bazenguissa-Ganga, Rémy, 'Les milices politiques dans les affrontements', *Afrique Contemporaine*, no. 186, 1998, pp. 46–57.

Bernand, Carmen, 'Ségrégation et anthropologie, anthropologie de la ségrégation. Quelques éléments de réflexion', in *La Ségrégation dans la ville. Concepts et mesures* (J. Brun and C. Rhein, eds), Paris: L'Harmattan, 1994, pp. 73–83.

Bouillon, Florence, 'L'après-guerre de Bosnie. Conditions de vie et processus de fragilisation de familles bosno-tsiganes dans une cité marseillaise', *Études Tsiganes*, no. 14, 2000, pp. 57–70.

Codhes, *Un país que huye. Desplazamiento y violencia en una nación fragmentada*, Bogotá, CODHES/Unicef, 1999.

Gomes, Nathalie, 'Solidarité et réseaux dans l'exil. Les réfugiés somaliens clandestins au Kenya et en Éthiopie', in *Populations réfugiées. De l'exil au retour* (L. Cambrezy and V. Lassailly-Jacob, eds), Paris: Éditions de l'IRD, 2001, pp. 301–19.

Hernández Delgado, Esperanza, and Salazar Posada, Marcela, *Con la esperanza intacta. Experiencias comunitarias de resistencia civil no violenta*, Bogotá: Oxfam, 1999.

d'Halluin, Estelle, *Guerre et psychiatrie. L'intervention humanitaire en Palestine*, Mémoire de DEA, Paris: EHESS, 2001.

UNHCR, *Fifty Years of Humanitarian Action*, 2000.

—— *The State of the World's Refugees* (annual).

Jewsiewicki, Bogumil, 'Pathologie de la violence et discipline de l'ordre politique', *Cahiers d'Études Africaines*, nos 150–2 (Disciplines et déchirures. Les formes de la violence), 1998, pp. 215–26.

Kibreab, Gaim, 'Revisiting the Debate on People, Place, Identity and Displacement', *Journal of Refugee Studies*, vol. 12, no. 4, 1999, pp. 384–428.

Le Pape, Marc, 'La Presse et les réfugiés rwandais au Congo-Zaïre (octobre 1996-août 1997)', *Afrique Contemporaine*, no. 183, 1997, pp. 57–66.

Malkki, Liisa H., 'Refugees and Exile: from "Refugee Studies" to the National Order of Things', *Annual Review of Anthropology*, no. 24, 1995, pp. 495–523.

Mohamed-Abdi, Mohamed, 'Les bouleversements induits de la guerre civile en Somalie: castes marginales et minorités', *Autrepart*, no. 15, 2000, pp. 131–47.

Ocampo, Francisco Taborda, 'De la infamia a la esperanza, la incertidumbre persistente: el caso La Miel', *Revista Foro* (Bogotá), no. 34 , 1998, pp. 12–17.

Pécaut, Daniel, 'Réflexions sur la violence en Colombie', in F. Héritier (ed.), *De la violence*, Paris: Odile Jacob, 1996, pp. 223–71.

—— 'Les configurations de l'espace, du temps et du subjectivité dans un contexte de terreur: l'exemple colombien', *Cultures et Conflits*, no. 37, 2000, pp. 123–54.

Peter, Krijn, and Richards, Paul, 'Jeunes combattants parlant de la guerre et de la paix en Sierra Leone', *Cahiers d'Études Africaines*, nos. 150–2, 1998, pp. 581–617.

Rancière, Jacques, 'Biopolitique ou politique?', *Multitudes*, no. 1, March 2000, pp. 88–93.

Vidal, Claudine, 'Le génocide des Rwandais tutsi: cruauté délibérée et logique de haine', in Françoise Héritier (ed.), *De la violence*, Paris: Odile Jacob, 1996, pp. 325–66.

INDEX

Q. John Fitch, who was a Bardstown resident, is recognized as being the first to conduct successful experiments with what mode of transportation?

A. Steamboat.

———◆———

Q. Kentucky Ridge State Forest is in what county?

A. Bell County.

———◆———

Q. What Louisville attraction exhibits over 1,500 animals in naturalistic settings?

A. Louisville Zoological Garden.

———◆———

Q. Farmland makes up what portion of Kentucky's total area?

A. Approximately three-fifths.

———◆———

Q. In the production of coal where does Kentucky rank nationally?

A. First.

———◆———

Q. Kingdom Come State Park on Pine Mountain features what 290-foot slab of stone that juts into the sky at a forty-five-degree angle?

A. Raven's Rock.

———◆———

Q. What park is on the site of the community of Rock Haven, which was destroyed in the great flood of 1937?

A. Otter Creek Park.

Q. Cave Run Lake was created by impounding the waters of what river?

A. Licking.

Q. Approximately how many acres of the state are covered with forests?

A. Twelve million.

Q. What record low temperature for Kentucky was recorded at Cynthiana on January 28, 1963?

A. Thirty-four degrees below zero Fahrenheit.

Q. The growing of dark tobacco in the southern and western portions of the state gave rise to what nickname for these areas?

A. Black Patch.

Q. Where did TVA complete its largest steam generating plant in 1969?

A. Paradise.

Q. What is the leading livestock product in the state?

A. Beef cattle.

Q. Situated in Fulton County on the Mississippi River, what is the lowest point in the state?

A. 257 feet above sea level.

Q. What is the approximate average annual precipitation across Kentucky?

A. Forty-six inches.

———◆———

Q. The domelike hills in north-central Kentucky give what name to the area?

A. The Knobs Region.

———◆———

Q. What is the estimated weight of the mass of suspended rock that forms the main arch in Natural Bridge State Resort Park?

A. Fifteen million tons.

———◆———

Q. The R. W. Robertson House in Paducah was once the center of what extensive dairy operation?

A. Edgewood Dairy.

———◆———

Q. Cassey Creek in southern Trigg County is noted for what type of fish?

A. Rainbow trout.

———◆———

Q. In what year was Mammoth Onyx Cave opened to the public?

A. 1921.

———◆———

Q. What city is the home of Ezra Brooks and Kentucky Tavern distilleries?

A. Owensboro.